HOW TO WIN FRIENDS AND TALK TO ANYONE

2 MANUSCRIPTS IN 1: IMPROVE SOCIAL SKILLS, BE MORE LIKEABLE AND INSTANTLY CONNECT WITH ANYONE

STEVEN HOPKINS

contained within this document, including, but not limited to,
— errors, omissions, or inaccuracies.

CONTENTS

HOW TO TALK TO ANYONE

HOW TO MAKE PEOPLE LIKE YOU

HOW TO TALK TO ANYONE

IMPROVE SOCIAL SKILLS, GAIN SELF-
CONFIDENCE AND BOOST CHARISMA
TO INSTANTLY CONNECT WITH
ANYONE

INTRODUCTION

Have you ever wondered how some people can talk to anyone naturally and effortlessly?

While you would love to go out and meet people, your poor social skill is stopping you from having the success you've ever wanted.

You want to build your social circle, create meaningful relationships and, maybe find the love of your life. You know that social skill is important for your success in life, but you are also terrified when you need to make small talk.

Maybe you've tried different methods of talking to people that have never helped. Perhaps you took an acting class, went to a speed dating session, or even talked to a professional about how to talk to other people. If after you've tried all this, and you still feel like you can't talk to people, maybe you would think, "So, there's no other way"? Well, actually, there is. I am going to show you exactly how to master small talk in this book, but before that, let me tell you a little about myself.

How I Transformed My Life

I was once a person crippled with social anxiety, but now, I'm happily married with two kids, and am a personal trainer, an entrepreneur, a life and motivation coach. What changed me? Well, one of the things that started my transformation was improving my small talk. Yes, sure, there were other factors that helped me, but these were linked to my self-confidence. My low self-confidence meant that I found it difficult to speak up and connect with others. Linda Vale, the woman who would eventually become my life coach, helped me to see that the separation of my parents, when I was six, had had a major impact on my life. I had fallen into a pattern of hiding myself away from others and as I grew into an adult my lifestyle choices meant that I wasn't in as great a shape as I could have been. I had become reliant upon frozen meals for dinner and got very little exercise. Certainly this was a reflection of how little I thought of myself.

My chance encounter with Linda, on the train home one night, made me look at my life in a different light. If you read my book: Self-Discipline to Exercise, then I'm sure you know my story. For years, I tried different practices, bought into certain "programs," and even took medication to improve my social anxiety. What I found works the most, however, is starting small. I've accepted the fact that there is no small fix. There's no pill that's going to make me the most intelligent person in the world that always has the best conversations, constantly making meaningful connections. I can't just turn a switch and change my personality.

I can, however, look inwards to determine what needs to be done to make me a more confident, happy, and healthy person. I understand now that talking to people is a practice, and some days are going to be harder than others. With the right methods, techniques, and practices, however, I know that I have the ability to talk to anyone. It's a freeing feeling and one that's like lifting a weight off my shoulders. I'm going to share my secrets with you now so that you, too, can have the ability to talk to anyone.

It can be hard to grow yourself. You might have to confront certain issues or recognize unhealthy behavior in order to improve certain aspects of your life. Some days, I just wanted to give up and lie in bed instead of head to a meeting where I knew I would have to do a lot of talking.

There was a time in my life when I was looking for a job, and I had a couple of interviews coming up. I would get so nervous before the interaction that I would feel sick to my stomach. I canceled an interview with someone, expecting that I just wouldn't get that job. The fear of the interview felt awful, and the negative feelings didn't disappear once I canceled the interview. They just manifested in other ways.

The person I was supposed to have the interview with reached out to me and ended up giving me a second chance. I went to the interview and nailed it, landing the job. The fear the first time around was bad, but the feeling of getting the job was great. I realized at that moment that confronting my fears was hard, but it was so much harder to continually live in a state of fear. Instead of being scared all the time, I now am only scared in certain situations. And when that fear creeps up, I have the tools needed to silence all the negative thoughts that might make me want to run and hide.

The Importance of Small Talk

The first and most important step on the road in learning to talk to anyone involves small talk. This is just the practice of general discussion with a person on the surface. Small talk can sometimes feel as though it's unimportant, but in reality, it helps to create the stepping stones that will lead to a greater connection.

Small talk is also an important practice in growing confidence. Even if you will never see that person at the coffee shop again, it can still be an important part in developing crucial social skills that you need in other areas.

Is This Book for You?

There's a reason you're reading this book. Maybe you've noticed work relationships lacking because you can't speak up and be confident with other people. Perhaps you're tired of being so afraid to leave your house because of the social interactions you might have to endure. No matter what you might be feeling, remember that you should be proud for recognizing that your social skills can improve. This book is for you, and it's going to help you achieve everything that you've wanted for yourself. If you can learn to talk to anyone, you can start to get what you want from others, create more meaningful connections, and improve your life altogether.

1

CONQUERING YOUR SMALL TALK FEAR

Courage is resistance to fear, mastery of fear, not absence of fear.

— Mark Twain

The thing we have to remember about conquering our fears is that the anxiety and worry won't go away; they just become easier to manage. For example, if you're afraid of flying but you have to travel for work, every time you get on the plane, you're still going to get scared, but by the 20th flight, you're a lot less worried than you were the first time around.

The way to learn to manage this fear is through practice. Start small by having conversations with people that you know well and trust. Be actively listening to them and yourself to make sure that you can pick up on what works and what might not through each conversation.

Change Your Limiting Beliefs

We often limit what we believe ourselves are capable of. We do this by limiting our imaginations, or denying that we are capable of more than what we see before us. This is something that I did again and again before meeting Linda, my life coach, and beginning my journey of transformation. I refused to see myself as anything other than an overweight guy sitting behind a desk all day and eating frozen pizzas for dinner. If you've read my book on how to build Self-Discipline to Diet, then you know what I went through to finally change that limiting belief and my identity.

Changing your limiting beliefs can be a first important step in overcoming your small talk fear. When you're overly invested in your own version of truth, you can really block a lot of people around you. To make sure that you're maintaining an open mind towards new conversations, you have to identify your own perspective and the boundaries that it might create.

Sometimes, we become so sure of our own realities because it's the most reliant thing we have. The world is so full of chaos and mystery that it's important to make sure that we have a solid set of beliefs and morals to give us at least somewhat of a limit on the things we do and think. Sometimes, however, this can be limiting rather than encouraging.

Embrace a Growth Mindset

To change your limiting beliefs, you have to embrace a growth mindset around conversations in general, including small talk. Stop looking at conversations as methods to get what you want. Don't avoid small talk with someone just because you don't think it will bring you any value. Every person has a different perspective so it's important to know people on an individual level, not a transactional one.

The best way to encourage your brain to continue growing is by reminding yourself that there really isn't a stopping point. There's no limit on all the valuable things that you know, so the more you open yourself to different experiences, the more you gain from each and every moment. Every experience, conversation, and moment we have, whether it's good or bad, is valuable. Even moments we sit in a waiting room for hours can add value, as long as we look for the importance in that experience. You might have a conversation in which you learn something, or you could help make someone else's day even better.

How to Stop Being Self Conscious

If only we had the confidence that we believe others have. The truth is, even the most confident, brave, and courageous people have moments of fear. Even the most famous pop star that belts her heart out on stage week after week might continually have anxiety or dread over the concerts, fearful of what could happen. Hard to believe, right?

Sometimes, you just have to let the act of confidence come before you feel it. There are going to be moments when you just want to run back to bed and hide under the covers, but you just have to put on your shoes, take a breath, put on a smile and face whatever challenges you have.

There's no quick pill you can take that's going to make you stop being self-conscious. Instead, you have to learn different methods that you can implement each time you feel like you might be having a self-conscious moment. Here are some tips that can help you get started:

1. Don't put people on a pedestal. At the end of the day, we're all individuals with good and bad moments, thoughts we wish we didn't have, and regrets we like to keep secret.
2. Don't say anything to yourself you wouldn't say to your best friend. You wouldn't tell your best friend that what they have to say is stupid, so why do you allow your mind to say that to yourself?
3. Cut out negative thoughts. Those thoughts have no value unless you give it to them.
4. Remind yourself that most people are just as self-conscious, if not more, than you. They're more likely to focus on their own issues rather than any small thing you

might have said that you believe to be embarrassing.

Small Talks Are Not Stupid

Sometimes, Small talk can feel meaningless, especially if you don't go beyond the current weather or what you might've eaten for breakfast. However, you have to remember that small talks are just the first step towards getting to bigger conversations.

Think of a relationship you might have with a small child or animal. You wouldn't walk up to them right away and just pick them up, hug and kiss them, right? It's tempting depending on their level of cuteness, but you would first probably crouch to their level, stick out a hand, and let them get to know you first. Think of small talk as this moment of letting them "sniff your hand."

Small talk serves a purpose for meaningful relationships. You might have met your friend in the strangest way without any small talk, but not all relationships will form in this way. Small talk is your chance to get a sense of what a person is like. Are they nervous, shy, or confident? Do they have a good sense of humor or do you need to be careful to not offend them with your jokes?

Practice Makes Perfect

The best way to practice having good conversation is to do them! If you have to, start online. Sometimes just getting involved in forums allows you to start practicing putting your thoughts into words.

From there, go outside and have conversations with strangers. It's the opposite of what our parents told us to do, but don't be afraid to start a conversation with the person in line at the coffee shop, or someone sitting next to you on the train. A lot of people don't want to be talked to, so if you pick up on the idea that they don't want a conversation, simply move onto another person. Don't force someone else to talk if they don't want to, so find people that actually want to have a conversation to practice with.

These methods of practice are easier because you know that if you do embarrass yourself, you might never see them again. Stop thinking and start doing, it's the only way for improvement to actually happen.

What we've learned

- Fear can sometimes be a manifestation of other fear. If you remind yourself to expand your mind and no longer have limiting beliefs, you can also overcome your fear of talking to other people.
- Your small talk fear comes from a place of being self-conscious. Overcoming your lack of confidence will make small talk so much easier.
- There isn't anything stupid about small talk. It is the way to get to more important conversations that will lead to stronger connections and relationships.

Making a good impression is crucial, and we'll go over that in the next chapter to ensure you leave a lasting imprint.

2

SEVEN SECONDS TO MAKE A GOOD FIRST IMPRESSION

Whatever makes an impression on the heart seems lovely in the eye.

— SAADI

Yes. You heard the title of the chapter correctly. It only takes seven seconds for you to make a good first impression. It might be in the form of a smile, or maybe in how you shake their hand. The first thing you say to someone could be important, or maybe they don't even hear what you had to say and instead just know they like you based on the warm tones of your soothing voice. There are many different ways to make an impression, but at the end of the day, the most important thing is making sure it's a good impression.

To do so, you have to first pay attention to your body language. You may or may not know this already, but your body language will tell the other person a lot about you. We don't all have to be body language experts to have the knowledge to tell if someone is uncomfortable or not. People who roll their eyes or avoid eye contact might be bored, or they could just be really tired. There are plenty of indications we can take from someone else in any given conversation, so we have to remember that other people have the same methods of understanding us as well.

This is something that I came to truly understand when I was making pitches for funding for different business projects that I was setting up. I could tell from observing body language, whether somebody was genuinely interested in funding me, or whether they were just being polite. It was during a pitch for one of my failed businesses, the line of gym wear, that I realized I had developed a sixth sense when it came to body language. It was also at this point that I realized the importance of my own body language.

The Importance of Making a Good First Impression

How many people did you meet once and form an opinion about? Sometimes, a first impression is all it takes for us to form the idea that we aren't interested in a certain person. While you can control whether or not you allow a first impression to define another person, you can't control whether or not someone is going to base their idea of you from a first impression. To make sure you're eliminating the chance of someone else disliking you after the first time you meet, you have to focus on making good small talk. In my book: How to Make People Like You, I go more in depth into the techniques and body language to make a good first impression, but for now, all you have to understand is how important it is.

The key to a successful small talk is a good first impression, and vice versa. You can't have one without the other. It can cause anxiety knowing that you could alter someone's perception of you within seconds, but that's why you need to make sure you practice different conversations to find what works for you.

First impressions have a significant effect on the future of a relationship. Whether we like it or not, people will form opinions of us right away. These impressions might eventually get proved wrong, or maybe it's just the way they see us forever.

When meeting people for the first time, you should strive to give them an impression of being friendly as well as approachable. There's nothing wrong with being too nice to someone the first time you meet them. Being "too nice," only becomes an issue later when people let others take advantage of them. Now, let me talk to you about some easy tricks you can use to make others like you instantly.

Dress the way You Want to be Addressed

Always dress respectably. The better dressed you are, the better impression you'll make. This doesn't necessarily mean wearing designer suits or dresses, but rather, putting effort into showing that you care about what you're wearing. When you give people the idea that you want to dress respectably and that you are trying to make a good first impression, it'll show.

Making an Impression with Your Clothes

Picking out what to wear is always specific to what the event is that you might be attending. Is it brunch with a college? An international conference? Maybe a first date with the lady or gentleman you met in a party? You have to gauge a situation before going to make sure you show up appropriately dressed.

Expressing Yourself with Your Clothes

To make people remember you, you can make an effort and express yourself with what you are wearing. However, be careful when you are attending some professional events. If you only like wearing tie dye, bedazzled, and ripped up clothing, that's great! But make sure you stick to something professional when the time calls for it. If you identify yourself with your clothes too much, people might make assumptions too fast about your personality and character.

Having an Open Body Language

If you're not careful with what body language you have, you could be sending the wrong message. It's crucial to become more aware of your body so that you can better evaluate how you might be giving off symbols in certain situations.

Stand straight. Not too stiff to where you look like a royal guard, but enough to where people can tell you actually care about being there.

Keep your hands visible. If people can see your hands, they'll be much more likely to trust you.

Have your shoulders relaxed. Tense shoulders create tense situations and can cause you unnecessary stress. Whenever you're talking to someone or even just when you're alone, check to make sure your shoulders are relaxed. Many of us don't even realize how much tension we're holding.

Share Your Smile With the World

When meeting someone new, a bright, genuine, and warm smile will always make things easier. Your smile is the greatest social tool you've ever been given. There are so many different situations that can be improved just with a smile.

A warm smile goes a long way toward making the right first impression. It shows you're friendly, likely happy, and welcoming to the new person.

A smile is a friend maker. You have the ability to make friends with anyone just by spreading a big smile across your face.

Eye Contact

Eye contact is always important when meeting a new person. If your eyes are shifty, people will start to wonder if they can trust you. If you can't maintain eye contact and instead are rolling your eyes or looking around the room, it makes the other person wonder if you actually care about being there and talking to them.

You don't want to stare directly into their eyes for too long, as it might make them feel uncomfortable, but you should do your best to try and maintain eye contact.

Handshakes

In any professional settings, understanding the art of a proper handshake is essential to making a good first impression. Your handshakes should always be firm. This might be the first impression anyone will have of you, so if you're too hesitant to shake their hand, or you let your arm hang loose, it might give them the wrong impression. You can really impress others with a firm handshake, but don't go overboard and try so hard that you break their hand.

Voice and Tone

Speak firmly. How you talk to others is the most important part of a conversation. Some people are soft-spoken and that's fine. However, be sure to keep a firm diction so that others can understand what you're saying.

Make sure you're loud enough to show confidence as well. If you're too quiet and people consistently can't hear what you're saying, eventually, they'll stop listening altogether.

Imagine one of several powerful people you know, do they seem confident when they speak? Do they speak firmly, with a high volume? If you can picture a person that fits this confident image, try to imitate this person when you speak. Observe the tone and voice when he or she speaks. Practice speaking with your partner, your family or a friend you trust. Believe me, you will start to speak confidently in no time.

What we've learned

- Your body language plays a huge part in the lasting impression you'll have on another person.
- Be aware of your clothing choices, how much you smile, what your voice and tone are like, and how much eye contact you make to make sure the other person is remaining engaged.
- Your first impression can define what the future relationship might look like, so it's

important to make sure that you're doing
your best to start off on the right track.

What's next? What should I say after that handshake, smile and eye contact? Well, don't worry. We
are getting there! You will learn how to properly
introduce yourself and make others remember you
in the next chapter.

3

HOW TO INTRODUCE YOURSELF

*Everyone you will ever meet knows something you
don't.*

— BILL NYE

Making an impression upon someone
is often down to how well you introduce yourself. Let's face it, we'll
never get another opportunity to make a first
impression on someone. It's important to
remember that while it can be helpful to develop a
consistent way to regularly introduce yourself to

new contacts, it won't work very well if it doesn't feel natural. The way I met my wife, Michelle, for example. Michelle met me at the gym where I was working as a personal trainer. She was looking for some hints and tips on gaining muscle tone, and I was happy to help. It was a natural setting, a natural meeting. There were no airs, or affectations and that is what this chapter is all about: introducing yourself in the most natural, but effective, way possible.

Greet Appropriately

A greeting is the very first step when a conversation starts. Even if you've seen someone around, it's always important to make sure that you have a formal introduction with this person. Shake their hand, look them in the eye and learn their name.

Like we mentioned earlier, smile is a powerful tool to make people like you. Greet a person with a friendly smile, and you are on your way to building a good new relationship.

Always follow the other person's lead when greeting as well. You want to make sure that you're not too overbearing in the beginning to where they feel uncomfortable, or so shy and timid that they don't remember you.

Make sure to first start by asking them how they're doing. Most people will say "good" or "fine," but it's not the words that matter. It's how they say these things. A rushed tone might mean they don't have time to chat. They'll probably say good even if they're feeling really down. You can base what you do next from how their voices sounded in the beginning.

Determining the Level of Formality

The formality of a situation is important in order to determine the appropriate greeting. Sometimes, you have to make sure to shake their hand and give a full introduction of your name and title. Other times might only call for a simple, "Hey what's up, I'm Steven."

In order to determine the level of formality, make a judgment of the situation. Are the people you're meeting important in maintaining your status? Maybe they're a client for your business, one of your bosses, or even your girlfriend's parents. If these people have deciding power over you in any way, you should give them a formal introduction. This doesn't always mean handing a business card over with a firm handshake. You just have to be appropriate and make sure that you're not coming off in any way that would suggest you don't care.

You can be too formal sometimes as well, which makes others feel as though you're a robot or unapproachable. To make sure you're not being too formal, always offer a smile and be certain to ask about them. Ask how their day has been, how their flight coming in was, or if they need something like a glass of water. Make sure that the other person understands that you care about meeting them while also assuring them you're an approachable person.

Introduce Yourself Properly

Introducing yourself goes beyond saying your name. Sometimes, if it's a situation in which you're meeting for the first time and they have no idea who you are, you might want to include a title, such as producer, business manager, or something else that allows the other person to associate you with a position. You wouldn't have to do this if you're meeting other friends or people that aren't affected by your job title, but in a business setting, it's good to make sure there's no confusion about who you are or what your purpose might be.

Your introduction should tell people who you are, and it should encourage people to engage with you. After the initial moment of sharing names, it's important to have a light conversation about who you are as well. You should first ask how they're doing, and when they ask you, always tell them that you're doing "good," "great," or "fine." I know some of you might think this is inauthentic, but when you think about how important the first impression is, I think you will agree with me on this point. After all, we can always turn to the people we already built a relationship with to express our true feelings. So, even if you're in a bad mood, you don't want to tell them you're doing "bad" right away, or else they might get the impression that you're a grumpy person, or someone who often complains. Instead, you could just say something like, "I'm great! I had a long flight but I'm very excited to be here."

Introduce yourself in a memorable way, and one in which people will like and appreciate you. You don't want to do all the talking in an introduction as you want the other person to get the chance to talk about themselves. You do, however, want to still make sure you're a part of the conversation as this might be the only chance you get to talk to someone. Don't talk over anyone, but make sure that the other person at least gets an idea or two about who you are and what makes you an individual.

Give Them a Chance to Introduce Themselves

The introduction is not complete without other people introducing themselves. Especially in a business setting, you might want to just start talking right away about work, so you can get things rolling. You have to be patient, however, and instead wait for them to lead the conversation. They might have just done a lot of traveling them-selves, so maybe they just want to get a drink at the hotel bar and have a chat for a bit.

Even in an interview setting, you might feel the urge to start talking about yourself and your quali-ties, but still ask how the other person is doing and give them a chance to start talking about themselves and their day. This helps make you look like an understanding person with good listening skills, whilst also giving both of you the chance to make a deeper connection before going any further with your relationship.

What we've learned

- An introduction is the foundation for how a relationship is going to be built. You have to make sure that you're properly introducing yourself, so the other person gets an idea of who you are.
- Make sure the other person has the chance to introduce themselves as well. You don't want to talk about yourself too much and not give them a chance to speak at all.
- Make sure you're judging the level of formality correctly. You don't want to make anyone feel uncomfortable.

You've learned how to introduce yourself, and now it's time to find some cool topics to talk about! You will find some great ideas of how to break the ice when starting a conversation. Head over to the next chapter to find out!

4

GREAT CONVERSATION STARTERS TO BREAK THE ICE

My idea of good company is the company of clever, well-informed people who have a great deal of conversation; that is what I call good company.

— Jane Austen

A good conversation starter can transform an awkward, stilted conversation into an interesting, enjoyable discussion. After all, who wants to talk to a boring person? When meeting someone for the first time, you might feel uncomfortable and afraid to speak. But hey, they might be just as nervous as you do!

So when this happens, we need someone to break the ice, and it helps to have a few ideas of good conversation starters.

This chapter includes nine different topics that would be good conversation starters. Within each topic, there are three different questions you can use depending on how close you are with a person. The first one is something you might discuss with someone you don't know very well, and the third is a good starter for someone you have more of a rapport with.

Chat with Them About Their Lifestyle

What plans do you have for the weekend? You could discuss your own plans, and also get to know them a little better based on their activities. If they say, "nothing," then you could start a conversation about how much you enjoy having weekends off, or maybe suggest a movie or show you like that they could watch during their downtime.

Do you have any pets? People love talking about their pets, so you can never go wrong with this topic.

What's something strange about you I could never

guess just from looking? People love talking about themselves, especially sharing small secrets that might ignite the curiosity of the other person.

Ask About Their Traveling

Michelle and I have done so much travelling and I just love it whenever anybody asks us about where we have gone because it gives us the opportunity to relive some great memories and tell some fascinating stories. People are always surprised when we say that we spent a year living in Singapore, setting up a consultancy there. Sure, not everyone will have a story like that, but everyone likes to talk about where they've been.

Do you like flying? There's so much to talk about when it comes to airports, planes, and flying in general. This is something many people relate to, and with this you can also chat with them about your most recent travel experience.

What's the last vacation you went on? Vacations are the greatest things in life, so people are going to love talking about the trips they've been on, or where they might be going.

If you could go anywhere, where would you go?

This is a great topic that could lead to endless conversation. With all the places in the world to go, you won't run out of ideas when you start talking about travel.

Technology Conversations are Always Relevant

What kind of phone do you have? There's a lot to be discussed with the little box in our pockets, so you could really carry the conversation far with just this small question.

Do you spend a lot of time online? The internet is filled with an endless amount of information. You can ask them about their online use, or maybe talk about their favorite sites or YouTube videos they keep up with.

What do you think the future holds for technology? The future of technology is a topic that we pretty much never stop talking about. What do you think about a smart home? Is blockchain the new Internet? Is AI a threat to humanity? It's always going to be relevant, and there's a lot you can connect to with another person.

Discuss Their Personal Style

Where did you get that shirt? Asking about someone's shirt, dress, or other piece of clothing, is a great way to get the conversation going. You could discuss how much you like the store they got it from, or maybe talk about other clothing items that are similar.

Do you like dressing up? If you're at a formal event, this is always a great question to ask. Most people will share that they hate wearing suits or tight dresses, so they'll be more than happy to talk about their distaste for dressing up.

What's a current trend that you can't stand? People enjoy talking about the things that they hate, so you could really open up a long conversation with this question.

Ask About Their Past

Where did you go to school? A lot can be learned about a person and where they might have gone to school.

Did you like growing up in your hometown? By getting to know someone's hometown and their opinion on it, you can really get to know a lot about them.

What's your most embarrassing memory? This is a great discussion topic. It can lead to a hilarious conversation that can really bring you and the other person closer.

Talk About the Future

Do you have any exciting things planned this month? Maybe they're getting married or going on a trip. Finding out what they're doing next can lead to a great conversation.

Does anything about the future scare you? The future can be scary, so this open-ended question could be relatable for many.

What's your biggest goal in life? Not only will you get to know a person a lot based on what their goals might be, but you can also lead the conversation to a great place. I, for example, love talking about the future, and that's because I found my passion by using the list of questions I share in my book: How to Find Your Passion. If finding your passion and purpose is something you're interested in, I think the book can provide you with some valuable insights.

Chatting About the Weather Isn't Always Boring

Isn't it a great day out? This is pretty basic but starting a conversation about the weather can lead to many other great topics as long as you can carry it further than just the temperature.

Do you prefer the cold or the heat? Everyone has an opinion about whether they'd rather be hot or cold, so this is a great topic that could lead to a lot of different discussions.

What's your most beautiful memory about snow? The snow can hold a lot of dear memories for people, so there's a good chance the other person has some experiences they can discuss involving snow.

Discuss about Books and Movies

What's the last movie you saw in theaters? This conversation can lead to the discussion of that specific movie, or just movie theaters in general.

Do you have a large collection of physical media? People love talking about their collections, and you can get to know a person really well based on what media they might own.

What's the strangest movie you've ever seen? This could lead to a really funny conversation, and who knows, maybe even a great movie suggestion.

Random or Weird Conversation Starters

If you could switch places with anyone in this room, who would you pick? A random question like this can let people know you're down to have a funny conversation.

If you could be famous for anything, what would you pick? You can get to know a lot about a person based on their various talents or different desires and wishes.

What one item would you take to the moon with you? This kind of question can lead to other funny questions about what you might do on the moon.

What we've learned

- How you start a conversation is going to be crucial in how the rest of your relationship is built.
- Practice different conversation starters so that you're prepared next time a conversation gets boring.
- Remember to talk about general things, and always ask questions to keep the other person engaged in conversation.

You have learned so much about how to make a good first impression and how to start an interesting conversation. You may not believe there's more to it, but there really is! Head on over to the next chapter where we discuss some important small talk tricks you'd need to understand and practice. You ready? Well, let's keep up the good work and keep learning!

5

WHAT TO SAY – SMALL TALK TOPICS AND TECHNIQUES

Small talk is the biggest talk we do.

— SUSAN ROANE

Sometimes, small talk can feel meaningless. It might involve the weather, or maybe just a small chat about the things that surround us. But think about this, the more you think something is meaningless, the more you are inclined to not do it. And you are here to learn the art of talking to anyone, right? Seriously, you have to get the idea that small talk is meaningless out of your head. Just think of it as a means to an end. If done well, a small talk can lead to bigger and greater things that you wouldn't have gotten to. So, with that said, let's dive right in and see what are other things you need to pay attention when it comes to small talk.

Discussing General Things

Bring up general topics when starting off with small talk. You don't want to get into the most recent political election, or the news about global warming right away. Instead, find something relatable on a human level to get things going. Often, this might just be the weather, the food, or the event you're participating, but that can lead to a greater discussion.

You might start off by saying, "Wow, the lighting in this restaurant is beautiful," which is a simple and general idea. The other person might just say, "Yeah," and then you both sit in silence until your other colleagues show up. Or, you can say something more open-ended, such as, "The lighting is beautiful in here. I would love to have something like this in my house." Then the other person might ask where you live, or you can start talking about the other style aspects of the restaurant you like. You could ask a question too like, "Have you been to this restaurant before?" or if you know they haven't, say something like, "This reminds me of a restaurant back home." All of these kinds of comments or questions could lead to a bigger discussion, even though you simply started off chatting about the place that you're in.

Ask Open-Ended Questions

Sometimes, it's easiest to just ask simple yes/no questions when getting into different discussions with new people. If you have the urge to ask a yes/no question, try to think of a way that you can turn it into one that forces them to give a longer response.

"Do you like sushi?" is answered with yes/no. "What kind of sushi do you like?" forces them to at least give a longer answer, even if it's: "I don't like sushi." This is still a chance for you to come back and ask more questions about their comment.

Talk About Relevant Things

While it can be tempting to just discuss the weather, try to find relevancy to what you're discussing. This will help you get closer to making an actual human connection with them. Instead of saying, "I wonder if the rain's ever going to let up," try asking questions or making more relevant statements, like, "Did you bring an umbrella?" Or "I wish I would've worn better shoes for the occasion!" Don't just say what everyone else is thinking. Instead, try to find relevancy in everything you decide to discuss.

Encourage others to talk

Everyone wants to be heard, so you can't go wrong when it comes to asking someone's opinion. Don't force the conversation towards anything political or religious. These kinds of conversations are personal and can make even those that agree on certain topics upset. If you can't think of something to talk about, just ask a simple question. You'll be surprised at how a seemingly trivial question can often turn into an engrossing conversation. It often worked for me when I was at a loss as to what to say next. Once, after a pitch for my energy drink, I accidentally ended up in the elevator with the guy I had been pitching to ten minutes ago. I didn't want it to seem like I had done this deliberately to keep pitching to him, and I struggled to find something to chat about. Eventually I blurted out that I would be pleased to be getting back to my wife who was expecting to soon give birth to our firstborn. I asked if he had any children. He did and was eager to share some advice with me. We ended up chatting all the way to the car park. No, he didn't invest in the energy drink, but he remembered me when I went in to pitch the gym equipment project I was working on, and he did end up investing in that.

Sometimes, we get caught up talking about ourselves. If you feel as though you've been doing most of the talking, try to turn your next comment into a question that can force them to add more to the conversation. For example, if you've been talking about the new car you just drove to your business meeting, ask the other person instead how they got there. Instead of making a comment about yourself, twist it into a question that can help you learn more about them.

Remember People's Names

When you can remember someone's name, it makes he or she feel more important. No one likes to be forgotten.

Mention their name often. If you forgot someone's name, listen for it in other parts of the conversation. Don't be afraid to ask for their name again and just apologize that you forgot.

A trick to remember someone's name is to make sure you know how to spell and pronounce it. Once someone introduces himself or herself to you, repeat his or her name several times in your mind, and link the name with the face.

People love to be called by their own name. So if you really can't remember someone's name, it's better to just admit you forgot their name and ask again rather than go weeks without remembering what to call them.

Stay Curious

When you aren't curious, the conversation dies easily. Continue asking questions and keep the conversation going so that the other person knows that you're legitimately interested in the things they have to say.

Curiosity makes talking to others meaningful. Learning about other people is important, but what we don't realize is that we can also learn a lot about ourselves from the conversations that we have with those around us.

Listen Actively

Actively listen to them talk and don't interrupt them while they're speaking. A person that interrupts others quickly becomes someone no one wants to have a conversation with. If you do accidentally interrupt someone, make sure that you apologize and give him or her the chance to speak. Then ask questions about what they had to say to make sure they know you're engaged.

The most memorable and popular people in the world are those who give their undivided and entire attention. If you notice someone else in a conversation is interrupting others, make sure that you stand up for those that get cut off, saying things like, "Let's hear what Susan has to say," if you noticed she kept getting interrupted.

Feed Their Ego

Make others feel as though their opinion is important. Sometimes, you might not totally agree with what they have to say. You should still remind them that their perspective is interesting and that their opinions are valid.

Feeding someone else's ego is complimenting them. If you make sure to build someone up instead of trying to find ways to break them down, they'll feel much better leaving the conversation.

Focus on Them

Don't get caught talking about yourself too much. Talking about ourselves is easy to do since we know our own mind better than anyone else. We still need to make sure that we put the attention on other people, giving them the opportunity to speak.

Avoid interrupting or trying to one-up the last bit of information shared. Don't turn a conversation into a competition. Just give them their chance to speak and listen actively so they know they have your attention.

Knowing the general rules of thumb of small talk is important. But maybe you're still looking for more ideas to make talking to anyone that much easier. Here's a list of questions for inspiration.

36 Small Talk Questions to Make Your Life Easier

1. What's the best-hidden spot around here? (or around your hometown)
2. Do you have a hidden talent not many people know about?
3. Have you ever received a piece of advice that still sticks with you?
4. What surprised you most about your current job?
5. If you could adopt an animal that isn't commonly a pet, what would you choose?
6. What's the greatest gift you've ever received?
7. What's a game that you love playing often?
8. If you weren't doing what you're doing now, what job would you have?
9. What do you remember most about your childhood home?
10. If you had a superpower, what would you be?
11. Do you remember getting away with

something you should have gotten in trouble for as a child?

12. What show is your biggest guilty pleasure?

13. Do you prefer working long hours within a few days, or do you prefer spreading the work out?

14. What's a song that you know all the words to?

15. If you could adopt any dog, what breed would you choose?

16. What's a movie that you hated that everyone else has seemed to love?

17. Do you like cooking? What kind of dish do you cook the most?

18. Would you rather go to a zoo, a museum, or a national park?

19. What's your favorite holiday?

20. If you could get paid a high amount no matter what, what job would you choose?

21. What's the strangest thing that you've ever eaten?

22. What's the oldest thing you own?

23. If you could go on a road trip anywhere, what would be your destination spot?

24. Have you ever endured what you believe

as a paranormal activity?

25. What's your favorite method of transportation?

26. Have you ever thought of an invention that you later discovered already existed?

27. What's the most insane thing a boss has ever asked of you?

28. What's something you hated as a child that you love eating now?

29. If you could bring any dead celebrity back to life, who would you choose? (don't ask about a dead person in general in case it brings up real-life past trauma)

30. If you could only listen to one band or musician for the rest of your life, who would you choose?

31. If you had to pick only one season to live through all year round, which would you choose?

32. What's a food that you could eat every day?

33. Do you have any good books or movies to recommend I watch or read next?

34. Who do you follow online most closely? (a celebrity they might follow on Instagram)

35. What's the last thing you regret

purchasing?

36. Who would you choose as a partner to go on a reality competition show with?

What we've learned

- Keep conversations general so that you don't have to worry about running out of things to say.
- Keep questions open-ended and avoid anything that can be answered with a simple yes or no. You want to make sure you're maintaining a conversation that won't easily fade out.
- Remember people's names and feed their ego so that they feel important in different conversations. The more emphasis you put on them, the better they'll be, and the easier they'll remember you as well.

Once you start off on the right track by making an important introduction, it's time to get deeper into making a more meaningful connection. The next chapter will discuss exactly how that can be achieved.

6

BIGGER TALKS AND CONNECTING WITH ANYONE

Making mental connections is our most crucial learning tool, the essence of human intelligence; to forge links; to go beyond the given; to see patterns, relationships, context.

— MARILYN FERGUSON

Y ou should strive for a place in which you don't worry what other people think of you and find methods to be comfortable with yourself. That being said, forming meaningful connections is still one of the most important parts of life. Not only do you learn more about yourself from interacting with other people, but you can also help others grow as well through your own individual connections.

By this point, you should understand the importance of small talk and some tools needed to make sure you get off to the right start. It's frustrating that I can't personally be with you in these conversations to make sure the right things are being said, but these tools will help you keep up with convos after starting the initial small talk.

Show Enthusiasm

You should look eager to talk to the person. Who wants to talk to someone who seems uninterested? Trying to talk to someone who doesn't have any interest in being there can be very challenging. Instead of thinking about good conversations and what they could add, the other person will instead be focused on how uninterested you are, worried that they're boring you.

Smile and make positive gestures often. Sometimes, we have moments where we might fade out, lose focus, or forget what someone said during a conversation. This is normal, and while you should be doing your best to make sure that you keep focus, a smile and a head nod is an encouraging mannerism that lets the other person know they still have your attention.

Face them and make eye contact often. You don't want to stare directly at them, as this could cause an awkward feeling and make them feel as though there's too much pressure to talk. Maintain a normal level of eye contact and do your best to not think too much about your "staring strategy." The more you focus on eye contact, the more you'll think too hard about how you should be looking at someone.

Make your voice tone reflect your interest in the conversation as well. Even if you feel a little tired, make sure to keep energy in your voice so as not to drain the energy from the other person as well. Always keep warmth in your voice to encourage them to keep talking rather than a tone that could be cold or dismissive.

You know already that it's important to show to others that you're interested in what they have to say, even if you're just pretending. Amongst with family members it keeps the peace. Amongst peers it means that you'll be listened to when you're talking. These were skills that I needed to master when it came to setting up my digital marketing consultancy in Singapore. Creating that atmosphere where my prospective clients felt listened to, and their needs understood, was essential to our success there.

Stay Current

Be up-to-date on what's in the news, as it helps in bigger talks. If you don't know anything about what current events someone might be talking about, it might be harder for them to find a relatable topic that the two of you can discuss. The more you know about what's happening in the world, the better you can keep up with a plethora of conversations. It goes beyond just knowing what someone's talking about as well. You should strive to have something to add to the conversation, too.

Alternatively, if you aren't sure of what someone is talking about, don't be afraid to ask them. A person you're conversing with might not feel like explaining the current situation they're discussing, but they could still offer up bits of information in order to help you at least have a sense of what they're talking about.

Don't be afraid to ask questions. It's always better to admit that you don't know what someone else is talking about rather than getting caught pretending like you know something you clearly don't.

Developing Your Own Value

You should aim to develop your own value and opinion about life, relationships, work, and other various topics. The stronger sense of self you have, the easier you'll be able to share bits of information about your personality and interests with others. People can see a big difference in those that have their own idea of what might have value versus someone that doesn't really have any solid opinions of their own.

Read books. Books will open the door to so many discussions in various conversations. Even if someone else hasn't read the same book as you, you both could find relatable key points in the discussions about a certain novel.

Travel when possible. Those who have traveled a lot have the ability to see many amazing things that others don't. If you have the financial stability to do so, aim to travel as much as possible. I can't tell you how much I learned from traveling. The things we saw and people we met in China, South East Asia and other places in the world we traveled to, taught me lessons I could never learn in books. By traveling, you can broaden your perspective on life and gain plenty of interesting experiences that will always be engaging conversation topics.

Connect with more people. There's a difference between knowing a lot of people and actually connecting with them. Focus on developing strong relationships with different individuals rather than just trying to be friends with as many people as possible. Having one strong friend is more valuable than 20 friends that don't even know your last name.

Constantly challenge yourself to go out of your comfort zone. The more you can force yourself into a situation that forces learning and growth, the more you'll develop as a person, therefore developing a stronger value and overall sense of worth.

Explore Topics

Don't stay on just one topic. When you find a topic that you both relate to, it can be tempting to just talk about this all night. Use that topic to help you explore other areas of a particular person's interests. For example, if you find out that the both of you are from a small town in Idaho, you might want to just talk about that all night. Then, you both just become the people from Idaho! Instead, ask where else they might have lived, or if they do some traveling. From there, you can branch into more topics as well. Keep the level of variety as high as possible in your conversation.

Find something the other person is excited about. If you bring up a topic and notice their eyes light up or a smile spread across their face, dive deeper into that topic. Notice when someone is passionate about a certain topic so that you can expand on that and create a more interesting conversation.

Ask a series of questions about the topic to show your interest. Even if you feel like you know something about a particular area of interest, you should still ask the other person questions to see what they know and if they have anything interesting to offer. You don't want to get to a place where you just school the other person on the things that they might like or care about.

Reveal Something Personal

Sometimes, we might feel the need to keep ourselves closed off so that we don't show too much vulnerability in any given situation. You should still aim to reveal something personal about yourself, as this allows the other person to feel more connected to you.

You might want to make it seem as though you aren't flawed, but perfect people aren't relatable. Show that you're human through your flaws or a personal bit of information.

Not too personal that will make the conversation awkward. For example, if the conversation moves to a topic such as baseball, maybe you had a traumatic experience as a child that caused you to absolutely loathe the sport. Instead of diving into a topic where you talk about your childhood trauma, just tell them that you just don't feel comfortable playing that certain sport.

Maintain and Deepen Conversation

Engage the other person and share relatable information about yourself, but make sure you listen at least as much as you talk. It's easy to talk about ourselves, but no one is going to want to listen to you sit there and do all the talking for hours at a time, so give them a chance to share the same amount or more information.

Respect the other person's opinion. Don't push people to see your perspective if you find that you are arguing. Though they might think Chicago pizza is better than New York, but you're an NYC native, don't get into a heated argument. Just agree to disagree.

Follow up the personal opinions or statement with relevant questions. Though their opinion might be different than yours, don't try to change it, just try to learn from it. Maybe they have a perspective you never even considered.

Ask more open-ended questions that dig deeper about things that matter to you. This way, instead of arguing about who's right or wrong, both of you are developing strong opinions.

What we've learned

- Show enthusiasm when talking to other people. No one is going to open up to you if you're acting like you don't care about what they have to say.
- Developing your own value is important in creating your own sense of self, which will also make small talk, and talking in general, much easier.
- Talk about things the other person is interested in, and maybe even reveal something personal so that the two of you can develop a deeper connection.

Being anxious is the quickest way to turn a conversation sour. The next chapter will discuss how to avoid this while providing important ideas to achieve a high level of confidence.

7

HOW TO STOP BEING ANXIOUS

Worry is a thin stream of fear trickling through the mind. If encouraged, it cuts a channel into which all other thoughts are drained.

— ARTHUR SOMERS ROCHE

Anxiety is a powerful emotion that can greatly affect how we react in certain situations. Some people only feel anxious when they have a big event coming up, while other people struggle to leave their homes due to crippling social anxiety.

The important thing to remember about anxiety is that it won't necessarily ever go away. Anxious thoughts will always travel through our heads, but we don't always have to give them the same amount of energy. Sometimes, you just have to let the feeling of anxiety run its course but remember that how you react to that anxiety is the most important part.

We've all been in a situation where we were anxious. Maybe it was sitting for an exam. Maybe it was attending a job interview. Maybe it was when you were on a date and you really wanted to impress the other person. Anxiety is something that has plagued me all my life, starting with the aftermath of my dad moving out of our family home. Luckily, there are ways to overcome it.

The best way to overcome anxiety is to practice mindfulness. Anxiety is fear over the future or remorse for the past. The different levels of anxiety are always varying among different people, but you should still be sure that you practice the same anxiety preventative techniques that psychiatrists recommend.

Mindfulness involves making yourself grounded and present in any given moment. If you focus on your surroundings instead of your inner thoughts, you can be more connected in the moment, leading to a better memory of the situation and more involvement with those around you.

Remember that everything takes practice, and this includes reducing your anxiety. You're not going to be able to go out right this instant and not be anxious in all your conversations, but you can at least start to recognize anxious patterns and determine the best course of action to combat these certain fears.

Maintain Posture

Confident body language does more than making you look good; it makes you more memorable. A person will notice if you're confident, and they'll associate that kind of trait with you more than if you keep yourself small and closed off, not being open at all with the other person.

Stand straight and avoid slouching when sitting, and let your arms hang naturally. The more aware of your body you become, sometimes it's harder to hold it normally, but always remember to make sure you have a body language that's inviting, not one that makes you seem unimportant or forgettable.

Develop a Sense of Confidence

Do not let the fear of looking like foolish keep you away from speaking up and asking questions, or telling your own stories, and sharing your own opinions. It's much better to say something that you don't feel confident about than to not say anything at all.

Stand and sit up straight and maintain eye contact both while listening and speaking. If you give off the idea that you're overly conscious of what you're saying and that you don't wish to share any of your own opinions, it's letting the other person know that they shouldn't hold any value in you either. If you can't love yourself, or see your own worth and value, how do you expect anyone else to see it?

Be Calm and Collected

Stay calm and composed all the time to handle conversations effectively. Even if you're freaking out on the inside, worried what to say next or trying to figure out what the other person might be saying, remember to keep your cool. The other person can notice if you're feeling especially nervous, and that's what can really turn a conversation sour.

If you notice you're getting nervous, focus on your breathing and listen to what they say. Practice mindfulness during conversations by watching the way someone moves their mouth, uses their hands, and what the look in their eyes might be representing. Don't focus on yourself, but instead, turn your attention to the other person. Even if you can't keep up with *what* they're saying, you can put an emphasis on *how* they're saying it.

Laugh Appropriately

Make sure the humor you use is relevant to the situation. You might think of a funny joke or remark, but before speaking, make sure that you're not going to say anything inappropriate. Ask yourself how someone could find offense in a joke before saying anything.

Laughing when you should show that you are confident and not nervous. Make sure you're not overdoing it, however, or else others might start to wonder if you're being genuine. Laugh when others do to make sure you're not sticking out too much as someone that just laughs because they feel uncomfortable.

Don't Be in a Hurry to Talk

Allow them to talk the most while you're egging them on. When you actually think of an idea or something to share, you might start to get the feeling that you just want to spill out all your emotions and feelings. Refrain from this and instead try to make sure the other person is getting their turn in any given conversation.

Avoid Fidgeting

Fidgeting is a sign of nervousness. While you might think others don't notice what you're doing with your hands, they can at least self-consciously pick up on your different fidgets. This might lead to them being nervous as well, or they'll just wonder if you're actually paying attention to anything that they're saying.

If you feel a need to play with an item or your hands, fold your hands instead. When you feel the need to shake your leg or sway from side to side, try going for a small walk, stepping outside for some fresh air, or changing positions. If your fidgeting feels uncontrollable and changing locations isn't an option, excuse yourself to the bathroom so you can take a few minutes to calm down alone. Practice some breathing exercises so you can use different methods to calm yourself down in times of high anxiety.

Keep Your Phone Away

Using your phone while talking to someone shows lack of confidence. It can be very tempting to just pull your phone out and start looking through social media when you're feeling uncomfortable. Don't do this in front of other people, as they'll either get the idea that you're self-conscious or that you don't care about what they have to say.

Using your cell phone is a distraction and can cause a loss of interest. Even if the other person has their phone out, you might still see something online that pulls your attention away, killing all the connections you've built up by simply showing momentary disinterest in the other person. Wait until someone is finished speaking or if you're in the restroom to check your phone. If you do check your phone in front of the other person, maybe share something you saw to keep the conversation going. No one is going to want to watch a video of something random off your phone, but you could check different news stories or updates, or even some photos you've taken and share this with the person you're talking to.

What we've learned

- Anxiety is a feeling we all have at different levels, but you must make sure that you don't let this rule your life.
- Stay confident even when you might not be feeling your best. You want to remain calm and collected and keep a steady pace with your talking, so others don't pick up on your lack of confidence.
- Don't fidget or play on your phone in order to make sure that you're staying fully connected to any given conversation.

Being calm and confident is crucial in any social settings. But some of you might have another question: how do I deal with the people I don't like?

Well, as Melanie Moushigian Koulouris once said:

"Everyone has a story to tell, a lesson to teach, and wisdom to share..." we should try our best to get to know someone before we start to judge that person. In the next chapter, we will discuss the importance of not casting too much judgment on those around you.

8

DON'T MISJUDGE ANYONE

If I stop judging other people, I free myself from being judged, and I can dance!

— PATTI DIGH

Unfortunately, many of us have fallen into a situation in which judging another person is easier than finding the good in them. We have all the tools it takes to pick someone else's actions apart, but when it comes to seeing the good in them, that can be a challenge.

Especially when it comes to ourselves. After the

failure of three different consecutive business projects I began ripping all my actions and decisions apart, but it was Linda, my life coach, who helped me to understand that there was more to their failure than what I was seeing. She, and Michelle, helped me to see the good in myself and that taught me to also see the good in others.

Know that the more you judge someone else, the more you're judging yourself. Your brain is trained to have certain thoughts, so if you put an emphasis on how someone looks or acts, it's a reflection on how you see your own looks and actions. For example, if you're constantly judging the shoes someone else wears, making assumptions on a person just because they're not wearing certain types of shoes, you probably put a lot of emphasis on your own shoes. Judging yourself too harshly can cause serious anxiety, so if you start going easier on others, you'll likely go much easier on yourself, too.

Don't Make Assumptions

Avoid making quick judgments about other people. Remember that the first thought you have isn't always the true view that you have. For example, a person might be wearing a dirty shirt that looks like it hasn't been washed. Your first thought might be, "Why couldn't they wear a nicer shirt?" But instead of coming to this conclusion, try to think of all the reasons they couldn't wear something nicer. Maybe they can't afford nice clothes and have to shop second hand. Perhaps their washer or dryer is broken, or maybe their house burned down, and they lost all their clothes. You never know what someone is going through, so you can't make assumptions until you know all the facts.

Be Open-Minded

Come out of your comfort zone. Though it's important to have strong morals and beliefs, you can't let these become strict rules for how you see the world. You should always be altering the way you think towards a more inviting path of growth and in a way that invites positivity and continual learning.

Be more welcoming to new ideas. Don't shut someone out of your life just because they seem like they might have a different perspective. You could end up learning something very valuable from them that you wouldn't know if you cut them out of your life.

Avoid criticizing them when they tell you anything personal. You might want to come back with a, "What are you talking about?" when they share that they don't like something you do. Instead, tell them something like, "That's an interesting perspective," making sure to not break them down for their thoughts and opinions. More often than not, they might not be that strong in their beliefs, and you could have some influence on that person if you stay positive instead of trying to "win" the conversation.

Look for the Good

Look for the good in people. Not the other way around. Our society has conditioned us to look for people's flaws, mostly because of the capitalist ideologies created by different advertisers. Practice looking for the good in the person, because even someone that you see as the world's mortal enemy might carry an important idea that could change the way you think.

Ask yourself questions about the good thing you can find in this person. Everyone has at least one good thing about them that makes them an individual.

What we've learned

- The harsher we judge other people, the harsher we judge ourselves.
- You can't assume anything about anyone, no matter what certain signs or signals they're giving off.
- The more open-minded you are, the easier it will be to keep a neutral perspective.

In the next chapter, we'll discover how to end a conversation in the right way to ensure that from beginning to end, you have a meaningful connection.

9

ENDING A CONVERSATION GRACEFULLY

People will forget what you said, people will forget what you did, but people will never forget how you made them feel.

— MAYA ANGELOU

It's important to remember that after you've finished speaking with someone, they're not likely going to remember everything that you said. They're going to remember certain ideas, but they don't have a script of all the different things that you specifically reiterated. Instead, they're going to remember if you were polite, funny, and generous, or if you were rude, cocky, and arrogant. It's important to not let yourself get hung up on every individual thing that was said and instead aim to make sure that you've managed to create a positive experience for the other person.

Say Thank You and Goodbye

Remember the guy with the baby advice whom I mentioned earlier? I was in the elevator with him and I asked about his children to make up a conversation that wasn't related to my pitch for investment. He ended up chatting with me and giving me baby-related advice all the way to my car. Eventually he wound up investing in a line of gym equipment I had designed. It was this incident that taught me the importance of leaving the conversation on a high. Because we'd had a good chat about his children he remembered me later on and already had a positive attitude towards me.

Ending the conversation can be very challenging, as you might not always know what to say. Always remember to say thank you to the person that you've been conversing with. If the conversation seems to be dying or the other person is losing interest, say something like, "Well thank you for giving me the time to talk today." This is also a great signal that the conversation might be over and it's time to move on.

Life would be so much easier if we could just walk away when we want to without having to go through all those goodbyes. There are plenty of people who will say, "I hate goodbyes," but seriously, who likes them? Goodbyes can be sad, awkward, and uncomfortable. In order to alleviate this tension, remind the person of how much you enjoyed their conversation. You can try thanking them with phrases like:

- It's been so great talking to you, I've really learned a lot.
- I appreciate that we were able to get together and have this conversation.
- I've enjoyed discussing different things with you and think you have a really great perspective on (specific topic).

End with a Handshake

Shaking someone's hand at the end of the conversation is a great way to give the person one last chance to remember you. It's a physical reminder of the time that you shared together and a great way to leave a lasting impression on them.

Always make sure that your hand is "shakable." Don't shake someone's hand when yours is covered in grease, food, or sweat. If you just ate a large meal and you know the night's coming to an end, go to the restroom to wash your hands just to make sure you're not going to leave them with the lasting impression that you have bad hygiene.

Your grip is important as well. Having a firm hand-shake is important, but you also don't want to be remembered as the person that almost broke their fingers. Always consider the other person's culture as well. If you're not sure what's appropriate, keep your hands available and lead them out the door with your arm so they know that if they wanted to shake your hand, they could. Some cultures don't find it acceptable for a man to shake a woman's hand, or for people to touch at all. If you're doing some international traveling, be sure to investigate what the proper handshaking moments are.

Referencing the Next Conversation

When ending a conversation, it's important to make sure that you're setting up the relationship for future opportunities. This might include simple phrases like, "I look forward to seeing you again," or it could be something more complex like, "We're still on for drinks on Thursday at 5:30, right?" You want to make sure your relationship is open for the next time that you can get together.

Even if you think it's the last time you'll ever see a person in your life, at least let them know that you hope to see them again by saying something like, "I hope to see you soon," or, "Let's keep in touch, so we can get together again."

Asking Questions

Sometimes, you might want to ask some questions when ending certain conversations. Maybe this will include asking them if they had a nice evening, enjoyed their meal, or if they need anything else before departing. Make sure that you're taking care of their needs even in the final moments that the two of you are together.

This shows that even though you're done with the conversation, you still greatly care about the other person and their needs. They'll be more likely to remember you if you give a clear effort in maintaining your relationships.

What we've learned

- Ending conversations are hard, but you should be prepared to make sure it ends gracefully.
- Practice handshaking to make sure that this moment of physical touch will help you leave a lasting impression.
- Always thank the other person for talking to you and remind them of when you might be able to have a discussion again in the future.

AFTERWORD

I appreciate your decision when choosing to read this book. I hope that you have learned some valuable information throughout this reading. Don't be afraid to reread any information you might have missed and take notes to make sure you're pulling the relevant and applicable information out, so you can reference it quicker if you must.

If you worry about starting conversations, write down some of the conversation topics or other questions to ask in order to have them handy when you're talking with other people. You might feel foolish having this tool with you, but there's no shame in being prepared for any conversation that might pop up.

Remember that the key to improvement still lies within yourself. As much as I would love to be in your ear during important conversations, I can't. You have to remember these techniques in order to use them when going throughout various social interactions.

I encourage you to practice what you have learned through the book. Remember that the key to talking to anyone is practice. Just like everything else in life. You aren't always going to win. Sometimes, you might have a conversation with someone and you go home, only regretting the things that you said or wishing you had even said more.

Once a conversation has ended, there isn't anything to do. If you do have regrets over certain aspects of a conversation, just look at it as a learning experience and not something to beat yourself up over. You'll get better at talking with each and every conversation you have. The most important thing to remember is that practice makes perfect!

I am always happy to give others the benefit of my experiences and knowledge, but I am also still learning as I go along. We are never done growing and developing as people, and this is an important thing to remember. So don't get down on yourself for turning to a book like this, a self-help book. Instead of feeling down, you should feel empowered because you are taking control of your life, identifying a weakness and trying to improve yourself. There is absolutely nothing wrong with that as that is the way I came to ditch my desk job, take up a whole new direction to end up with the job of my dreams and the family of my dreams. With the right tools and exercises, you can achieve your dreams too.

HOW TO MAKE PEOPLE LIKE YOU

PROVEN STRATEGIES ON INSTANTLY ATTRACTING OTHERS AND WINNING THEM OVER

INTRODUCTION

Have you ever wondered why some people are liked and popular while others are not? Well, I want you to know that most of these people know some secret techniques and have successfully applied these techniques to get to their current positions.

What are these secret techniques? As a reader of this book, you will learn what these secrets are and how to apply them.

You might be wondering why you need people to like you. Shouldn't you just 'be yourself and not care what anybody thinks'? Well, think about it this way. We all need people in our lives. Whatever we do in this world, whether directly or indirectly, we want someone to notice and acknowledge it.

Almost everything you can be is dependent on the relationships you build, and when people like you, and you make connections, you will be welcomed with open arms.

Making a new friend, meeting your future in-laws, acing an interview, winning an election, or wooing a partner all depend on people liking you, and this book is structured in a way that makes difficult things easy to understand.

My life has been aimed at helping people. As a life and motivation coach, I specialize in motivation, self-discipline, communication, NLP techniques, psychology, and human behavior. I have been really fortunate to work with so many people either as a personal trainer or coach, helping them discover the secrets of winning, and it all begins with getting people to like you.

I have worked with a lot of people with different backgrounds, beliefs, and professions, and my long years of practice have taught me that everyone has a "soft spot" which they are fond of, and once you can find what that soft spot is, you can access their hearts.

Sometimes I look back and I still can't believe that I once moved my family around the world to start up a digital marketing consultancy business in Singapore. It seems crazy now, but we moved out there knowing just a handful of people, and most of them were business contacts. They were very polite but the relationship wasn't destined to go any further than our business dealings. We had to make friends if we were going to make a real go of living and working there. Michelle is great at making friends and a lot of the advice and suggestions I make in this book come from what I have observed of her. So a lot of the credit must go to her, I suppose!

I have given many seminars, coached, and talked to different groups of people and individuals from different walks of life, and it has been a very exciting and rewarding experience.

To further reach and help more people overcome the different challenges that they face because they can't build proper connections with other people, I have decided to take the advice of friends, colleagues, and people I have worked with and write a book to guide and coach people on the secret of "how to get people to like you."

How to make people like you is an interesting topic I discovered while growing as an entrepreneur. I eventually realized that the art of getting along with people in everyday business is a calculated fine art. The most interesting part is that the topic can be taught and learned.

The human body holds a lot of secrets that, when properly used, can speak volumes and can be used to make total strangers feel comfortable around you while you build rapport.

It is interesting to know that a few gestures and body movements can make people form an impression about you, and when you follow up with a little conversation, you can convert a total stranger into a friend and get them chatting.

Why do you need to read this book? Well, I have a better question in mind. Who doesn't need friends and meaningful connections in life? You will agree with me that in any profession you find yourself, what you need to succeed are people.

While building relationships comes naturally to

some people, for some, it is almost an impossible task.

For any of the categories mentioned, the techniques discussed in this book are applicable to all to either improve your existing skills or to learn from scratch how to get people to like you.

Why is it important to be likable?

First, you should understand that being likable is no special inborn gift, but a skill set. And it is learnable.

Here are a few things you need to know about people that are likable:

- People that are likable get elected and promoted more than people that are less likable.
- People that are likable have a more successful life and career. They get easily rewarded and are more popular.
- People that are likable are better salesmen; they close more deals and make more money.
- People that are likable are mostly happier

and probably even live longer. Why?
Because they get more attention and
better service from other people like
doctors and other professionals.

According to a Columbia University study by
Melinda Tamkins, the success rate between some
colleagues in the same workplace is not guaran-
teed by whom you know but by how popular
you are.

The study showed that people that are likable are
seen as trustworthy, decisive, and hardworking.
They hardly miss out on opportunities as they
received recommendations.

The less likable people are more likely seen as
arrogant, manipulative, and conniving. They are
hardly recommended for any promotions or pay
raises, no matter what their education qualifica-
tions were.

When you are likable, a lot of things seem to fall
into place by themselves. And since likeability is a
learnable skill set, you will be on your way to the
top after you finish reading this book.

What makes people likable?

After realizing how being likable has a huge impact on your success in life, you wonder, what makes a person likable? Well, simply put, it is their ability to consciously connect with other people and always leave a better impression about themselves.

This book will help you awaken those abilities of yours that you have failed to put to use. Moreover, this book will help you discover, develop, connect, and put to good use those dormant abilities. In the following chapters, you will learn how to make a good first impression with your body language, how to master small talks, how to develop incredible charisma, and so much more! Now, let's dive right in and start learning about the first, and most important step to make people like you: making a great first impression.

1

MAKING A GREAT FIRST IMPRESSION WITH YOUR BODY LANGUAGE

We don't know where our first impression comes from or precisely what they mean, so we don't always appreciate their fragility.

— MALCOLM GLADWELL

Why First Impressions Are Important for Any Relationship

You might be wondering why you never got a reply to the text you sent to the lady or guy you met at the party last night who you were so sure you had a good conversation with. If this happened to you, or you have been in this kind of situation, then it is time to ask yourself if you created a good first impression.

"Was it the outfit I wore or something I did?" you may ask yourself. As a matter of fact, first impressions matter a lot as they create a lasting image of how someone sees you.

The people we come into contact with every day, ranging from people you say hello to at your office, at the gym, school, to the waiter at your favorite breakfast spot, could be a potential friend, someone you might need help from, or even a lover/spouse. You make contact with these people not even realizing what a brief interaction can bring about tomorrow.

Every contact comes with a great opportunity for what may be tomorrow, but the key to deciding on whether the meeting will materialize or turn into something bigger is the first impression you make.

Let me illustrate this with an example from my own life. As a young entrepreneur trying to get projects off the ground I wanted to put myself in a position where I was earning more money for my young family, especially with our firstborn, Sammy, on the way. I had some ideas for health drinks and gym equipment and needed to get private investors on board. One of the guys I went to meet at his office, didn't end up investing in the idea I had first presented to him, but we ended up in the elevator afterwards and chatted about children. He was only too happy to impart some advice and although the business meeting had officially ended in his office, this ending in the car park was very positive and we both remembered it. The next time I went to him with an idea in need of funding, he already had a positive first impression associated with me.

Now you should start believing the saying that a first impression is always important, and we don't get to make another.

The Power of Nonverbal Communication

Since more than half of communication is through body language, this is a very important subject. At the end of this section, you will understand the power of nonverbal communication and why it is so powerful.

Nonverbal communication is usually the way you look, listen, react, or the signs you give a person to show if you are following the conversation, agree or disagree with a proposition, and whether you care or not.

In a situation where you are conversing with someone and what you are saying matches with the nonverbal communication you make, it builds trust and a relationship. And if it doesn't, there might be confusion or tension.

For instance, when you are sitting in a cafeteria and someone walks up to you to ask if the seat next to you is taken, if your answer is "No" with your head nodding, you might sound dishonest. And, with nonverbal communication being a natural language that transmits your actual feelings, the person will likely go with your nonverbal connotation.

In order to show your true intentions, make sure your nonverbal language is well utilized during a conversation. When it is well utilized, you look more honest, confident, lively, and likable.

So instead of just saying "No," you can add more body language by smiling and using other parts of your body.

Smile

I know you feel this sounds so simple and might be wondering what a smile has to do with people liking you. Here is a fact you have to know: smiling is a powerful way to easily make people like you.

Maybe you would think that smiling all the time is simply inauthentic, but think about this: when you smile, you immediately create a bond or connection between you and the other person, making the person glad to talk to you. It does the magic by sparking some kind of a pleasing response from the person involved, and this can also come in the form of a responsive smile.

Smiling is a trick I always use that has worked countless times. Since I know people generally believe smiling is contagious and would rather be around someone with a cheerful and beautiful smile than the person giving a stern look, why not just use the trick in your favor?

This is very important because you feel connected to a smile emotionally and physically. Also, the brain releases endorphins whenever you smile. This triggers a feeling of peace and happiness.

Many times, people link this feeling with the personality responsible for it.

So, if you don't have a smile on your face or lack the skills for one, it's time to devote some quality time to your mirror by standing in front of it and learning how to smile. If you are around people, whenever possible, try as much as possible to smile, and you will soon find out how simple yet effective it is just to put on a beautiful smile on your face.

Make Gentle Eye Contact

To create a first impression when you want to make people like you, making eye contact plays a major role, and it is a big step to take. With the use of gentle eye contact, you project great confidence that is generally perceived as attractive.

On the other hand, people who are not able to look others straight in their eyes are seen as dishonest, untrustworthy, and lacking in confidence. Just imagine: if you are talking to someone and you hardly see this person's eyes, wouldn't you find this person untrustworthy and simply don't want to talk with him or her anymore? If you agree with me, pay attention to your own eye contact when you are talking with someone!

I believe that eye contact brings about trust and indicates honesty and sincerity—and we all know that getting someone to like you involves making that person trust you. Therefore, keep that in mind when you are trying to connect with anyone.

To practice eye contact, find a person you can trust and let him or her know that you are trying to improve your communication skills, then, try the following strategies:

1. Establish eye contact right away: establish eye contact even before you start talking.
2. Use the 50/70 rule: to avoid staring and making the person feel uncomfortable, maintain eye contact for 50% of the time while speaking, and 70% of the time while listening.
3. Look from side-to-side: if maintaining eye contact is too difficult to you, try to look into that person's eyes and hold it for 4-5 seconds, and then slowly glance to the side.
4. If you can't maintain eye contact, you can

also look at an eyebrow or the space
between the eyes and mouth.

5. Avoid looking down: doing this can give
   an impression that you lack confidence.
   Tell the other person to let you know if he
   or she sees you do this.

6. Practice: it is natural for some people to
   establish eye contact. However, it's okay if
   it doesn't come naturally to you. Keep
   practicing, and remember to remind
   yourself to maintain gentle eye contact
   whenever you are talking to other people.

Mirror their body language

Getting people to like you can be somewhat tricky,
but if done with the methods I have put together, it
becomes easier. It has worked for me, my clients,
and a whole lot of other people.

When making a first and lasting impression, you
can employ the use of mirroring the other person's
position. It is a proven fact that people tend to like
those that are similar to themselves.

Take your time to observe someone. If you realize
the person you meet is quiet and calm, you should

also find a way to act that way. If the person likes smiling, give him or her lots of smiles too. And if you meet a person that talks a lot, try to keep up! Trust me, I have used this technique to make a lot of friends.

Always check the person's posture and gestures to know how to act. Is the person feeling relaxed or uptight? Is he or she looking nervous, tense, or anxious? Study them carefully to match the position. This will make them like you subconsciously because they feel that you understand them or are similar to them.

Make Physical Contact

Over the years, the psychology of physical contact has been a fascination for researchers and people in general. People are curious to know why physical contact can be so influential.

You might be asking yourself questions like "How does simple physical contact make you do something you never thought you would?"

To be honest, it has also been a fascination for me and I believe it must have crossed your mind too. The truth is: when physical contact is made, oxytocin, serotonin, and dopamine, which are also called the "happy chemicals," are released inside the human brain.

The reaction triggered by the "happy chemicals" lowers the level of cortisol, which is the stress hormone. The lowered cortisol levels make you feel relaxed, slow down your heart rate, and reduce your stress level. Invariably, physical contact can trigger comfort.

With a lot of studies backing up claims that a simple touch can greatly affect and boost your chances of having your way with people, it is a strategy to put into practice.

Most communication is made through physical contact. Just think about it: physical contact is involved when you offer someone a handshake, when you pat someone on the back, or give someone a bear hug.

When you touch someone, they don't notice it easily, but a reaction is taking place inside their body. A simple touch can put the person in the mood and can immediately spark a relationship since he or she will be feeling relaxed and interested in hearing what you think.

At the end of it all, you have to coordinate your body language to gain that good first impression and trust. So smile, make gentle eye contact, mirror their positioning, and touch them if you need to.

When getting someone to like you, your aim at creating a relationship is to share a common ground. I believe this chapter has been able to clear up some misconceptions about a first impression and has pointed out why it is very important to make a good one. In my book, *How to Talk to Anyone*, I talk more in depth about first impressions and how important they are when you want to build a long-lasting relationship with someone.

The next chapter involves verbal communication. There, you will be learning how to use powerful small-talk techniques to make people like you, almost instantly.

What We've Learned

- First impressions are crucial for any relationship. If you can make a good first impression, everything else will become easier

- Employ the power of nonverbal communication (smile, eye contact, physical touch etc.) to enhance your relationship

2

POWERFUL SMALL-TALK TECHNIQUES

*Communication - the human connection - is the key
to personal and career success.*

— *PAUL J. MEYER*

S ometimes, small talk can feel meaningless, especially if you don't go beyond the current weather or what you might've eaten for lunch that day. However, you have to remember that small talks are just the first step towards getting to bigger conversations. Here are a few useful techniques to master the art of small talk:

Ask people about themselves

It is good that you have created a first impression with someone you just met, and you were able to use the right body language and coordination. You smiled and made gentle eye contact, fair enough; you followed through with mirroring some of their traits like positioning, and it worked. Good for you. Now that you have succeeded in attracting their attention, what next?

It's time to follow up with conversation. To create bonds and build trust, having a good conversation is key.

Who Can Engage in Small Talk?

If your personality is that of an introvert, there is a big possibility that you are not a big fan of small talk, and people might get the wrong idea about you, thinking you don't like other people. But as we both know, this is simply not true. You just have to conquer your limiting beliefs and practice.

Remember, conversation is a two-way thing and you need to do the talking and the listening at the same time. Anybody can become an expert at conversation; you can master small talk once you understand the techniques to apply.

As you read on, you will find handy techniques that can help you sail through that awkward silence, especially in a situation where you suddenly become tongue-tied instead of building the intended rapport.

Let me tell you a story. I remember one time during my college years, I was riding a bus, and sitting next to me was this beautiful lady who looked like a really interesting person. She had a lovely smile on her face.

I wanted to start a conversation with her, but then I was suddenly overwhelmed with this feeling of self-consciousness. So many thoughts started running through my mind: "Am I good enough to talk to her? Will she find me interesting? Will she ignore me? Where do I even start?"

These types of questions can make you feel tongue-tied and lose the rapport you want to create. Eventually, I didn't even get a chance to talk to this lady, and that was all because of my fear of small talk. After that, I made a decision to overcome my inner fear, and built strong self-confidence to be able to talk to anyone.

So where do you start? Well, if I can give you one piece of advice, I would say that the secret to keep a conversation going is to get the other person talking.

Ask More Questions

A good way to get the conversation rolling is by asking people questions about themselves. This is really effective, especially when you really don't know what to say. Get the person talking and make them share the things they like most, what matters to them, and things they consider as their favorites.

A proper conversation is a two-way street. Asking about the other person is a way of showing interest and a good way to learn and even hear a story about their experiences or their past. Questions are rather non-judgmental inquiries, and most people let their guard down when they sense care or concern from your questions. Besides, people generally like it when they are the center of attention. Hence, you make the other party feel good about themselves.

In the realm of small talk, the most important thing to remember is when to stop talking and start asking. From the responses of your partner, you pick clues and hints to be able to decide when it's time to stop talking.

Try to ask the other person's opinion about things and compliment them when necessary. Let's take the example of my business meeting for funding that ended up with me chatting with the guy about babies in the car park. That came from his willingness to share advice and my willingness to sit back and let him talk. I asked him questions here and there but nothing too probing. Instead I let him reveal himself.

When asking questions, remember that there are two ways to ask questions – the open questions that demand a long answer and the closed questions that mostly require a "yes" or "no" answer.

It's better to go with the open questions that will get the other party talking for a while, so you can listen more and show that you are interested in them. The spotlight will be on the other party and you can probe more. Be conscious of closed questions as the short answers might leave you struggling for the next thing to say.

Talk About what interests the other person

When you talk about what interests the other party, you will probably get them going on and on, taking the pressure off you and giving you enough room for the next question. To begin the conversation, find common ground, a general topic that can connect both of you and which you can both converse about.

The occasion for the meeting will determine the tone of the conversation. For example, "The hall looks well lit, don't you agree?" "Beautiful weather tonight, isn't it?" "The program was really awesome. How did you feel about it?" "My wife is a great fan of your work. How long have you been writing?" All these questions are preparing the conversational ground.

Good follow-up questions can be "Who do you think plays better?" "Where can I get something like this?" "What do you think about the performance tonight?" Hearing your question, the other party will be inclined to give you a long explanation because your question is an open question and it concerns what interests them.

Lead the conversation

When the other party feels they are in charge, make them believe they are truly in control; that way you can steer the conversation in any direction you want.

However, the key to keeping open questions flowing is using the *'Who, Where, What, Why, When, and How'* method to maintain the tempo and length of the conversation.

When you apply the open method of questioning, you will surely find out what they are interested in. Questions like, "Where do you think that came from?" "How do you want this to be?" "Which one would you recommend and why, please?" Yes! These questions will surely leave the other person with no choice but to offer an explanation, description, or to tell a short story.

Use their Name or Nickname

People love hearing their names. At every good opportunity, try to call them by their first name or nickname and you will be creating the opportunity for them to like you since you are feeding their pleasure centers.

When people hear their name, it will further draw them in and reward the pleasure centers of their brain. People love it when they hear the sound of their own name; it can make the rapport you are building take sudden shape. When you call out their name, you are telling them how important they are, and they will most certainly be interested in you. They will remember how you make them feel, which in turn makes them feel happier and reassured.

By subconsciously planting positive feelings in someone when you mention their name, they will form an impression of you and feel you are connected to them in a positive way, and that will amp up your likeability level.

Bring Along Your Sense of Humor

People pay money for others to make them laugh; you can see that happening at stand-up comedy shows and when clowns are invited to events.

A sense of humor can actually improve your like-ability. It is human nature, and also logical that humans would rather be around those who make them feel happy and good. A good sense of humor can help you get on the good side of many people.

It's Hard to Hate a Jokester

Cracking a joke or two is a smart way to break the silence, get people to relax around you, or create a lasting impression around new people. For example, maybe you mentioned your name earlier to someone, but this person just didn't remember your name.

The other person might politely ask, "Sorry, I'm quite terrible with names; what was your name again?" Maybe your name is Paul Coleman. You could create a little humor by saying, "I'm Paul Coleman, but my friends call me PC." You could add, "When you hear them call me PC, you might even think I build them, or I'm a walking personal computer. Don't be deceived though."

Seeing you as someone who has a carefree approach to life will get most people to smile and call you that name your friends call you. They are telling you they also want to be friends by calling you "PC" instead of "Paul Coleman."

Most People Like a Room Filled with Laughter

The most liked people are those who can keep the room lively and filled with laughter. Regardless of how people picture their ideal friend or romantic partner, they will always be comfortable around someone with a sense of humor.

A study from researchers at DePaul University and Illinois State University found that when you are first getting to know someone, using humor can make the other person like you more. The study further suggested that participating in humorous tasks together can further increase romantic attraction, quicken the bond of friendship, or get people to easily like you.

Laugh easily and smile often

When you smile a lot and laugh openly, you can easily win people over. Giving a big and natural smile when you meet someone for the first time will mostly guarantee that they will remember you later.

I had two home teachers when I was a kid; one often smiled when he taught and would politely call my name before he explained whatever I didn't understand. It was easy for me to understand whatever he taught me and I always looked forward to his lessons.

The other teacher was not as friendly as the first. He never smiled, and it felt like he hated me, or he at least hated teaching me. Well, as a kid I naturally developed a resistance to him and I preferred to spend more time with the teacher who smiled. I would rather ask him about things I didn't understand than ask the other home teacher.

Make People Feel Good

Since people are different, how can you know how to make them feel good about themselves? Well, it is quite universal because people prefer to be perceived the way they see themselves. Everyone has their own beliefs about themselves and their perceived selves are aligned to that.

The universal characteristics of everyone include wanting happiness, more attention, love and care, and being useful and productive. When people get those vibes, they will surely like you.

This experience is described by the self-verification theory. Everyone wants confirmation of our views, positive or negative.

They Feel Good; You Feel Good

When you talk about people and they feel good about themselves, they will feel good about you. However, watch what you say. You don't have to be unduly positive, or else they might feel you are either naïve or just overly flattering them. Intelligently comment on the good you see and avoid talking bad about things or people.

When you complain about others, the impression you give your listener is that they may be your next victim to lose your respect and end up being in your negative book. It goes further as they might also link your complaints with your character and view your complaints as your true self.

Tip: Never ever badmouth your former employer, no matter what previously happened. This is something you should take note of, especially during a job interview.

Compliment Them

Everyone has an image of who they feel they are and sharing compliments with them can really make them feel good about themselves. If you do so, the bond between you and the people you meet will increase. Sounds simple right? Sure, it is. People love a well-timed, genuine compliment, but there are ways to go about how you dish out those compliments in order to leave your conversation on a more positive note.

The key to perfect compliments is not to be false, but genuine, a little bit unique, and well timed.

Be Specific

When you give compliments, don't just tell the person, "You are gorgeous." Tell them why you think they are gorgeous. "The dress is a perfect match for you and you really look gorgeous in it." This type of compliment is specific and based on experience and fact, and people will be inclined to like you more.

Praise Their Efforts

People love validation, whatever field it may be in. After exhausting lots of efforts, nothing beats being acknowledged and getting a compliment.

Don't just say, "Nice speech." Tell the person why you think the speech was nice, because he or she may have exhausted a ton of effort to put the talk together. "You delivered a nice speech. I really love that point (fill in the blank) that you talked about."

When you give compliments, always give the reason why you feel that way or why a person deserves the compliment.

What We've Learned

- Getting people to talk about themselves is a terrific way to keep the conversation going.
- Calling people by their name creates a sense of importance.
- Everyone is naturally drawn to a calm and relaxed environment. Make people comfortable by complimenting them.

3

START WITH YOURSELF

Friendship with oneself is all-important because without it, one cannot be friends with anyone else in the world.

— *ELEANOR ROOSEVELT*

Like Yourself

Before getting people to like you, like yourself first! For people to like you, you need to get busy liking yourself. However you treat yourself is how other people will see you. So basically, you attract what you are.

Once you love yourself, you will attract the same

force, attracting more love into your life, and getting more people to trust you.

With the years of experience I have gathered in psychology, I've come to realize that it is difficult to get anyone to like you if you don't possess the characteristics of self-love. How can someone like you when you don't feel happy about yourself? Well, I don't blame them if they don't; no one wants to associate with a sad fellow.

Self-love gives you inner peace, fulfillment, and contentment. If you have self-love, you are happy with yourself and your life generally.

Have you heard a story of someone who claimed to be rich, but who ended up committing suicide? It's sad and is something that always shocks me. There isn't a single one of us who is immune to the impact of low self-esteem.

I went through a lot of failure before finding the keys to success that I am sharing with you now. Working my dull office job, before I became a personal trainer, was something that brought me down every single day. Similarly, suffering failures years later, with the gym-related business products I tried to market, I was brought low. I had a baby on the way and needed to make more money. There are few things more heartbreaking than knowing you cannot provide enough for your family. When you begin to feel down, you start to see all your failings and it snowballs into a bigger malaise.

I have come to realize that most of the people that fall under this category are people that don't have enough self-love. They see their life as an act, harboring negative thoughts that overpower their clear judgment.

Have you ever been around people and felt you need to talk less to be noticed due to feeling intimidated? Or have you looked at yourself in the mirror and felt you are looking too fat or too slim? You are not alone; I have been down that road too.

Seeing too many flaws in how you naturally look will lower your self-confidence and your thoughts might become negative. You are not better off doing that; rather, take action and love yourself more.

Never allow those thoughts to influence how you react. You should act on thoughts that will bring out your true self. Change what you can about yourself and let that confidence show. Apply a zero-tolerance to any form of self-critique.

Also, forcing yourself to be someone you are not won't do you any good; rather, focus on yourself and make yourself happy. Once you start forcing things, people around you will notice, and it will be too obvious you are acting as something you are not.

Practice Personal Hygiene

The topic "personal hygiene" is an important one to discuss in this book as it can help some people that face challenges making friends due to negligence. I will have to be candid as I proceed—you will have to pardon me! But trust me, it will do you a whole lot of good.

So, our parents were right, after all. Practicing good personal hygiene not only promotes good health but has other benefits in life. Bad personal hygiene can repel people—and I don't blame them after all.

Just put yourself in their shoes. If someone you know hasn't had their bath or smells, I am sure you will try as much as possible to avoid that person, right? So you understand how important it is to keep yourself nice and clean.

We all need to wash our hands, bathe regularly, and brush and floss our teeth to help keep viruses, bacteria, and illnesses away from our body. This entails keeping good personal hygiene, and not only does it have its physical benefits, it also has its mental benefits.

With proper personal hygiene, not only will people see you as clean and tidy, but you will also feel good about yourself. A person with bad personal hygiene normally has a bad odor coming from his or her body or mouth, disheveled hair, and tattered clothes—and oftentimes faces discrimination from people.

On the good side, some people practice great personal hygiene in their daily life. Effortlessly, they brush their teeth, have their bath, see their dentist for routine checkups, and always wash their hands before eating. So, you see, if they can do it, so can you.

You can start by bathing and washing your hair regularly. Our body constantly sheds skin as some of the skin needs to come off to avoid caking and causing illness. Shave off some of that hair if you need to; clean and cut your nails when they are long; brush and floss your teeth, and at regular intervals, use mint gums or a breath mint.

Normally, you are supposed to brush your teeth immediately after every meal to reduce the accumulation of bacteria in your mouth. This bacterium can cause mouth odor, tooth decay, and gum disease. However, you should be able to brush at least twice daily.

Making it part of you might not be easy at first, but with dedication and persistence, it will become part of you. Also, you can start using a deodorant if you don't have one, and change your clothes every day.

Once your inner and physical body is well taken care of, the next thing to look forward to is the way to dress. Before stepping out, always look in the mirror to check if you look good and feel confident about yourself.

Dress to Impress

This might sound so cliché, but it is definitely something that comes in handy to know. The way you are dressed is the way you will be addressed. My teacher might have said that line again and again, but I only understood the true meaning of it when I started meeting people in places I wasn't familiar with.

If you have ever raised an eyebrow when you see someone wearing tattered clothes or mixing different colors that are too bright, you are not the only one. I am also guilty of this. On a more serious note, you will appreciate a well-dressed man more than a man that is scruffily dressed.

Dressing boosts your confidence

I remember that feeling I have when I know I have outdone myself and dressed better than other days. I smiled more, talked to people more, and was more than willing to make new friends. That was my confidence talking.

Dressing well will boost your confidence, not just from putting the right outfit together but from the compliments you will receive from people and the way they will stare at you. So, have you realized why you need to dress well?

Dressing creates a first impression

First impressions do matter a lot. By now you should know why it is important to create a good first impression for people to like you.

You shouldn't just dress how you feel, but you should dress the way you want people to see you. If you portray yourself as an unserious person with your dressing, people will take you that way, and if you are looking serious, people will also take you seriously. That's how our dressing addresses us.

Dressing reflects your personality

Of course, our dressing reflects our personality. A banker can't be dressed as a factory worker, nor can a doctor dress as an athlete.

I was guilty of not paying attention to the way I dressed until I realized we are judged on our clothes. Before I could be taken seriously, I had to dress to look serious. At first, I was reluctant to always take note of my dressing before I went out to seminars and lectures, but I later found out my dressing also speaks to the audience.

Opinions are formed in minutes, or even seconds!

There are times when people, without even knowing who you are or anything about you, jump to conclusions. Yes, I know it is not ideal to judge people without giving them a chance, but think of it, the human brain is wired to pick clues and inference from what it can see.

Hence, if you already gave a horrible impression through your clothing, you might not even be given the chance to correct it. Are you going to rush to change your clothing?

I guess not!

Hence, your dressing speaks highly of who you are, reflecting the kind of personality you are. This in turn makes people decide if you are worth a friend or not.

Wear Clothes That Fit

You shouldn't just wear clothes but endeavor to wear ones that fit. Some people get comfortable wearing clothes that are bigger than them. It might be a convenient thing to do, but it doesn't present you in the best way.

Wearing a size ten when you are a size nine will

not look good on you. It will look loose and shabby, and it won't fit you. On the other hand, clothes that are too small will only end up showing most of your body parts, and it doesn't look professional or comfortable either.

Go for clothes that are well tailored to your body type, and people will start thinking that you are a person with good taste and end up liking you.

Buy quality instead of quantity

A lot of people are of the opinion that having plenty of stuff reflects comfort. Well, I beg to differ; that is not the case. When we have few but quality things, it makes our life more organized and simpler.

It's better to opt for quality clothes instead of buying heaps of clothes that will soon get worn out and which you will end up disposing of. You should invest in quality clothes that reflect your style and personality instead of buying loads of clothes all in the name of having many.

A less complicated lifestyle will do you a lot of good. Embrace the mindset of a simple life, seeing fewer things as more.

Dressing to impress doesn't mean that you have to wear one style of clothing all the time, but rather, wear something that fits, makes you stay confident, reflects your personality, and creates a good first impression on the people you meet.

Spend time with people who improve your image

It is a sad truth, but as humans, we all tend to be judgmental; we easily evaluate someone we meet in just seconds. The same thing applies to you. Bear in mind that people you meet evaluate you immediately. They may be right or wrong with their results, but it's just how the human mind is wired.

Just imagine a mathematics equation that looks difficult at first glance. Most of us won't attempt it because we have the notion that it is difficult to solve. The same concept applies to people. We write off what we don't like. If you've ever found yourself in a situation where you are being criticized, you might be indirectly/unknowingly responsible for the criticism.

You are judged by your company

The ancient proverb, "birds of a feather flock together" provides a terrific explanation of the fact that people with common attributes move together. In other words, people that share similarities are inclined to always spend time with each other.

We get judged by the kind of company we keep. If you hang out with a group of geeks, there is a high chance that you will also be seen as one even if you are not. Also, if your choice of friends always look tattered, it will be difficult for people to separate you from them even if you are the neat one.

To sum up, your choice of friends should always portray the image of how you want people to see you. Otherwise, you might be misjudged by other people.

What We've Learned

- Liking yourself is the very first step to get others to like you
- Take time to look after yourself. You can

do this by practicing personal hygiene and wear clothes that fit you and of high-quality.

- Concentrate on being around people that challenge and improve you

4

THREE WAYS TO DEVELOP INCREDIBLE CHARISMA

Charisma is the fragrance of the soul.

— *TOBA BETA*

There are some people who just seem to have that "thing". When they show up in a room, when they are talking, when they are speaking in front of people...they seem to have "something" that just make people like, respect and listen to them. What is that?

Well, it's something called "charisma", and that's exactly what you will learn to develop in this chapter.

Generally, people perceived as being charismatic

possess some unique characteristics that are dynamic, powerful, and charming.

People with charisma have the power to draw other people close to them and to sell their ideas effortlessly. They have the aura to be in charge and command a room.

Charisma is not inborn but something that is learned. No matter the level of success one attains in life, charisma has played an important role in attaining that feat.

Often, it is believed that people that are easily likable are born that way. But have you thought for a second that each and every one of us can actually possess charisma? Here is the thing—there are some methods that can be applied to your lifestyle to make people perceive you as influential, responsible, honest, and trustworthy.

In this chapter, we will be discussing the three ways to develop incredible charisma.

1. Be Present During Conversations

Seeing charisma as the power to outshine others or look better than they are is far from the true meaning. Being charismatic is not about boasting about your good qualities but rather about making other people feel good and well listened to.

The true way to display charisma is to always make other people feel important, and when they have a conversation with you, they will feel better knowing they have your attention.

When you are in an important conversation with someone and you notice he or she is looking distracted and you hardly have his attention, I can imagine how angry and upset you feel about that. You are not alone in this. I have also been in such situations, and I am sure that I have been like this to others before.

I discovered through my discussions with my life coach and mentor, Linda Vale, that I had held on to the sadness of my parent's divorce since it happened when I was six. Linda helped me to realize that it was this fear of being abandoned that led me to push people away from the outset, and this extended to all my conversations and interactions with others. Luckily, she helped me realize what I needed to work on, and now I listen to others with all my attention.

Have you experienced this before? When you are talking to someone, he or she just seems to be distracted and is not really listening.

If you feel bad when in that kind of situation, also imagine putting someone in the same situation. If I am not mistaken, you won't run to the person who doesn't seem to be present during a conversation to pour out your heart next time. It suggests you no longer trust the person.

No matter how insignificant the conversation is, always put your full concentration into it by being present.

Focus your energy on the person to create a feeling of importance

If you want to get the person engaged and create a feeling of importance, then your mental and emotional energy will be put to use—focus it on them. As we discussed earlier, people have an affinity for being recognized and known.

For this to take place, you don't have to go out of your way. Create situations to make the person feel happy and confident. When they feel all this, it makes them feel important and eager to engage more with you.

Practice effective eye contact

I have come to realize that people who make use of eye contact in sending a message are seen as being honest, confident, truthfully, charming, and hardworking. These results aren't just the reaction you get; the quality of your conversation is also improved.

There is power in the eyes as they convey a message that will allow the receiver to feel heard, more connected, and positive about the message.

To practice eye contact, pay attention to whether you can hold gaze with someone during a conversation. When talking, tilt your head forward and look the person in the eyes. This will make the other person feel important and he or she will be inclined to trust you more.

People like attention... so give it

No one will be comfortable talking with you when

you are looking out the window or hardly concentrating.

Presence lies in the mind. You cannot give full attention to a conversation when your mind is somewhere else. To give your full attention, concentrate on the sensations you feel and use them as a point of contact.

The sensations can be your hands touching the table you are seated at or the shoes you are wearing. Just take a moment to concentrate on them to let them constantly remind you that you need to be present.

Keep your devices out of sight

I don't know about you, but I definitely don't like talking to someone that has headphones on or whose phone rings every second.

Putting your devices on vibrate doesn't solve the situation; you should keep them away to reduce the urge for you to check them at any given opportunity. That also tells the other party that you are giving him or her your full attention.

Try it! Next time you are talking to a person, turn

your phone to vibrate and put your cellphone in your bag. You will be amazed how this simple act changes the whole conversation.

Be expressive with your body

Using eye contact is not the only way to show your presence. You can use body language. There are gestures you can use to show this—nodding your head and doing thumbs-up to show agreement.

However, be careful to not overdo this, since overdoing this can reduce the person's perception of you. Only use your body language at the appropriate time for you to be taken seriously.

2. Develop a Sense of Confidence

You can easily build and maintain your confidence by regularly working out, feeling and looking good with your dress sense, and indulging in talking about things that you understand.

Individuals with charming personalities are usually very powerful. Although it doesn't mean that they have to be the leaders of the free world or the heads of a large organization,

Being powerful means you have the ability to bring about a positive change to your immediate society either through your physical capability, intelligence, know-how, wealth, or fame.

Become physically fit

People will notice the shape of your body the very first time they meet you. Looking all muscular and fit will quickly pass a message across to the most primitive parts of the other's mind about your potency and strength.

Your physical build or fitness also sends messages to people that you can withstand undue fatigue in the course of trying to achieve a certain aim and objective. No wonder we see men with an average-to-husky build tend to earn more than their out of shape and thin contemporaries.

With evidence to back this assertion, the *Wall Street Journal* reported on a study that found average-weight men earn more than their skinny peers. Therefore, if you want to be more self-confident, make sure you spend some time taking care of your body shape.

Have a purpose to live for

Confident and charismatic people always have a purpose in life. They have leverage and the ability to make a positive impact on their immediate society. There is a general impression that powerful people can easily get things done.

With the proper charisma, people will be easily attracted to you like a magnetic force or gravitational attraction. The root behind a magnetic force of attraction is power. Comparing it to the era of ancient cavemen, survival then depended greatly on congenial interaction with those at the top of the social hierarchy because they were the ones that could offer protection, food, and a mate.

For better survival, we need to set a goal, initiate an innovation, have a vision, and follow it with full dedication. People always want to have something to have faith in. If you want to make your dreams reality, then you need to strongly believe and hold onto them. Always have confidence in yourself in any situation.

Create the impression you know your endpoint even if you are not completely sure of the outcome. Leave people with the benefit of the doubt.

Feel confident and powerful

The act of being powerful has to do with your mindset. In fact, that is the starting point. You will carry others along if you show bravery and strength. As the saying goes *"fortune smiles on the brave,"* you have to be brave and confident to become fortunate.

When you are self-assured, you will always draw people close to you in the quest of trying to know you well.

The act of developing confidence is a gradual process that deserves to be given its own accolade. You should also know that the end goal of developing confidence is mastery. When you master anything, the way you think and go about things completely changes.

Whenever you are not sure of the destination, take advantage of whatever comes your way. Even in the moments when we do things we wouldn't normally do, we should always continue to thrive and excel.

3. Know how to talk effectively

If you find it difficult to start and maintain a conversation, you will need creativity. Think about it: what are the things you like from a person you so much admire? What will he or she like to talk about?

A charismatic person has a way with words and knows how to talk to people. Starting a conversation, leading the conversation down the right path, and getting people involved is effortless for them. If you don't know how to do this, then you need to start practicing.

Here are a few tips that you can use to improve your conversation skills:

1. Organize your thoughts: think before you say anything. If you can organize your thoughts, what you say will make more sense to your audience.

2. Be concise: don't use a lot of words to describe something simple. Ask your friends and family to give you some advice on this.

3. Be real: each of us is unique. When you are speaking, you should be natural and let the real you come through.

At first, it will be difficult, but once you are determined, and with lots of practice, you will get better at it. There are many groups, such as ToastMasters that are dedicated to improving your speaking skills. If you don't know where to start, look for a supportive group near your area and start from there.

Use humor as a tool

A person that knows how to sustain a conversation also knows how to make people laugh. Once you can make them happy, they will like you.

Share stories and experiences by using humor. If your story is not that funny, tell it in a way to make it sound funny. Before you tell a joke, think it through because it will be embarrassing to tell a joke and have it fall flat.

However, if that does happen, don't let that discourage you. Just remember that practice makes perfect. If no one laughs when you tell a joke, change the way you tell it and try again next time. Eventually you will find your own speaking style and develop strong charisma.

Ask questions

Asking questions doesn't show that you are dumb. Rather, if you ask questions, it gives you control. To show charisma, ask smart questions.

People that are curious to know more, and who ask questions, are usually portrayed as being intelligent. It is interesting to know that people who ask many questions give the best impression.

Think about our teachers in the classroom. They always tend to ask questions even when they know the answer. We see them as all-knowing and devoid of any fault. Being charismatic is getting to know others more than yourself.

The interviewers we see on TV ask a whole lot of questions of their guests but are hardly irritable since they are good with humor—and viewers love them for that. They seem in control and come across as charismatic individuals as they do their job.

You can only know how someone feels if you go close to them. Ask them questions to understand, know where they are coming from, and how they feel.

In conclusion, having charisma is not innate—you are not born with it. It is something you learn. With the three methods I have provided – be present, be confident and develop your communication skills, I believe that you will become a charismatic person in no time.

After reading the above techniques, make sure you put them to practice until they become a part of you. Once you master charisma, you will be able to wield power and have positive effects on people.

What We've Learned

- Being charismatic naturally draws others to you
- Be present and attentive in conversation—that includes your body, soul, and spirit
- Be confident and have something you believe in as your driving force
- Know how to make people feel comfortable around you

5

HOW TO ATTRACT AND MAKE GREAT FRIENDS

Some people go to priests, others to poetry, I to my friends.

— VIRGINIA WOOLF

Be yourself; everyone is unique

Being unique is a great way to get people to like you, and in order to be unique, you need to be yourself. There are no two people on earth who are exactly the same; we are all unique in our own different ways.

Everyone has different behaviors, personalities, beliefs, and ways of doing things. When in the midst of friends, show them what you've got! You don't need to pretend to be another person just to fit in; rather, show your unique skills and you will be surprised at the way you gain acceptance. One thing I know for sure is that people that exude confidence are easily liked.

In our world today, it is always a challenge to be yourself, especially when we see conformity as a norm. Well, the good news is that you don't have to try to join the majority; you can choose to be yourself and still attract great friends.

It is when you are unique that you attract terrific people who are genuinely attracted to the real you —the potential in you. And the fact is that you are more likely to attract and retain friends when you are yourself rather than when you're trying to be another person. This is because people see you as who you are; there is no need to wear various masks just to fit in and please people.

Set your standards and don't over-please people

It is not a bad idea or a wrong thing to try to please people, but it shouldn't turn out to affect you negatively. When you want to do something that will please a friend, acquaintance, family, or your boss, you are not in any way doing the wrong thing at all. However, note that in the course of trying to please the people around you, you might also, in turn, be going out of your way.

People with standards are seen as highly principled and well respected by their peers. Don't get me wrong: it is never a bad idea to please people— just don't overdo it. The people you are trying to please might start finding it irritating and less attractive when you are not confident of your standard.

When you have standard, there is a huge chance you will attract people who find you charming; people who are wowed by your standard. And best of it all, this might be the criteria for retaining great friends. Don't forget the saying, "birds of a feather, flock together." Hence, with your standard, you will likely attract and retain friends who are fascinated by it.

If you find yourself in a situation where you are feeling shy or not capable of saying no to a friend or a family member who always ask for money from you, then you should know you will be giving that person more opportunity to demand more from you. Always let them know how you feel and where you stand on things.

There is no way you are going to be mentally alert when all you do is try to please everyone close to you with your precious time and energy.

One major advantage you stand to gain when you take a stand is that you will be seen as being responsible. Everyone likes responsible people as they are easily trusted and can take charge of everything easily.

Take good care of yourself

Some of us find it very difficult to live a healthy life, which is one of the things people look at when they are trying to get to know you.

Apart from the fact that staying healthy is a vital aspect of getting people to like you, it is very important if you want to live longer and have a happy life. Staying healthy is not only good for your physical health but also good for your mental well-being.

I don't want to associate with an unhealthy person, and neither do you. Hence, these are the basic things we need to set in motion in trying to attract great friends.

Exercise

One of the easiest ways to keep fit and healthy is through regular exercise; the benefit of regular exercise cannot be overemphasized. There is a need for everyone, regardless of their gender, age grade, or physical strength to exercise in order to keep fit and look attractive.

A person who exercises regularly will feel better about their physical appearance, and this can help boost their confidence and self-esteem. When you go to the gym, for instance, you can form acquaintances with other gym members, and that might later develop into great friendship.

As a former personal trainer and current gym bunny who still takes pleasure in helping others to reach their exercise goals, you'll appreciate that I am a huge proponent of this. However, it might strike you as being a little vain. Surely people should like you for who you are, not what you look like, right? Yes, I'm all for that and I believe that we should not judge people on what they look like, but we're humans and we can't help doing it. It's human nature to judge on looks, and for the purposes of making a good impression it's important to look good.

Dress well

We discussed first impressions in the early part of this book. One of the criteria with which first impressions are judged is your clothes. The way you dress says a lot about you and can determine the caliber of people that are attracted to you if you attract them at all.

Hence, if are you on a quest to attract friends, be mindful of how you dress. It can determine if you will be successful in making friends or not.

There is a general notion that how you dress is how you are addressed. This means that if you want to be addressed in a respectable way, then your dressing should command respect.

Whatever occasion you are attending, dress for it. Take note of what you are wearing before you step out of the house, and once you feel comfortable and confident in what you are wearing, then you can step out.

Practice personal hygiene

We have talked about this earlier, but I want to talk more about personal hygiene because it is so crucial when you want to make friends. This is one of the most important factors you should take care of in a bid to getting people to like you. Take care of yourself, practice personal hygiene, be clean, dress neat and decent. Spend time taking care of your hair and bath at least once daily.

We have talked about why you should dress properly in some sections above. In addition to proper dressing, keep yourself neat as well.

Besides the fact that good personal hygiene is pretty important to health, it does have a long way to go in your bid to make people like you. I am pretty sure you will not be comfortable talking to anyone with an unpleasant body odor. These are simple issues you should be mindful of and pay attention to in order to attract awesome friends.

Let's talk about some good personal hygiene habits.

Make it a habit to clean up every morning. Take a good thorough bath. You will feel good and confident about yourself before going about your daily activities. If you are a victim of body odor, have a good deodorant on. Keep in mind, how you present yourself (in terms of overall body hygiene) determines the kind of people you attract.

The gums and teeth are also susceptible to bacteria, so there is a need for us to always keep them clean by brushing them at least twice daily. To get better results and avoid tooth decay and gum disease, clean your teeth after breakfast and before retiring to bed. Do not forget to brush your tongue if you suffer from halitosis.

Try and maintain a low cut. But if you do want to keep your hair, make sure it is tidy. Invest in a good hair cream and hair shampoo. An unkempt hair is an invitation to dandruff.

Also, form the habit of washing your hands at intervals. This way, you limit your susceptibility to diseases and germs.

Make sure you wash your clothes with soap and water before wearing them again. One other easy way of getting rid of disease-causing bacteria is to dry your clothes in the sun. The sun will kill the germs.

The mouth and nose should be covered properly with a tissue while coughing or sneezing to avoid the spread of communicable germs in the air and food.

When you devote time and energy to taking care of yourself, you will attract great friends. You will give out the vibe that you are responsible enough to take care of yourself; hence, sustaining a relationship won't be an issue.

Once the aspect of your personal hygiene is well taken care of, then you should aim to exude positive energy whenever you are around people.

Exude positive energy

A positive thinker attracts good friends because they focus mostly on doing things that bring out the best in them.

Consistent positive thinking can actually reflect in

your life, thereby becoming a part of you. This means that what you think about every day is what you turn out to be. So, if you are mindful of your day-to-day thoughts and avoid any kind of negative thoughts, people will want to be around you because they believe the positive energy will radiate into their life. After all, who wants to be around someone who is constantly complaining or saying bad things about others?

Believe in yourself and others. Practice positive thinking, and I am pretty sure you and your positive energy will attract amazing friends.

Be a Friend too

I know quite a lot of people who complain they don't have friends. When I talk with them, I discover that they are not so great at being a friend, let alone maintaining friendship. You can't expect a friendship to last if you don't make the effort to nurture it. Invest your time, your emotions, and yourself as well. Good and genuine friends are not easy to come by. Hence, you have to present yourself as a friend to attract and retain great friends.

It is not always easy to have a friend, especially a

good one. You will have to take your time to develop a strong friendship because it deserves every bit of effort. To be a good friend, always be supportive of your friends and be true to your word. You will soon find that you are surrounded by positive and genuine people.

Join groups to meet people

Not just joining any group, but the right one, is a good step to take when trying to make friends. You will meet people with different views and interesting ideas that you can make friends with.

I talked about the gym in a section above. This is a terrific place to develop acquaintances that could lead to great friendships.

If you are a Christian, for instance, when you join a group or subdivision in your local assembly, you may develop great friends.

Put yourself out there. Go and participate in different activities. You won't get to meet new and interesting friends if all you do is stay at home all day doing nothing.

Move past small talks

Don't get me wrong; I am not against small talk. But when it gets too lengthy, it becomes agonizing.

Move from small talks to deeper conversation. Be quick in asking someone you meet for the first-time deep questions so that you will be able to understand them fast.

You should also try to use deep questions to find out whether this is a person you really want to make friends with.

When you pass the conversational level of small talk, you are creating a bond that will leave a permanent impression on your counterpart. And if that happens, I am pretty sure the other person would love to have a conversation with you again.

In my book: *How to Talk to Anyone*, I teach people how to master small talks, how to move from small talks to "bigger" talks and develop long-lasting relationships. This is an important skill to develop because in the end, we want people not only to like us, but also to become our friends or even a long-term partner.

Display vulnerability

Showing vulnerability doesn't mean that you are weak; rather, it is a great way of getting acquainted with each other.

Opening up and disclosing the areas you are not too knowledgeable or comfortable talking is a good way to build a relationship.

Again, being vulnerable doesn't imply you are weak. It shows you have the courage to be who you are. Once people see your vulnerability, they will also open up to you and let you in on their secrets.

Value the time with the friends you have

Friendship, just like every other relationship, needs nurturing. You have to invest time and consciously make the effort to keep in touch. If you do not nurture it, you should not expect it to survive the test of time.

If you want to keep lasting and good friends you should try as much as possible to always be in contact with your friends frequently, no matter the distance. Thanks to technology, we can use social media to get in touch and schedule visits.

We should let our friends know that we value them. We don't need to be close to each other in order to value our relationship. A simple text message or call can always bring us together.

Connection leads to meeting new friends

Once you put all these tips into practice, I am pretty confident you will become a likeable person. If you are already a likeable person, with the tools and mindset I shared with you, people will enjoy your company even more.

Keeping in touch with old friends and connecting with them will provide the opportunity for meeting new friends. Keep in touch with your friends and always find time to hang out together.

Also, when you have the traits of a likeable person, you are likely to get invitations to places where you can meet other new people.

What We've Learned

- Everyone is unique. Be yourself and improve on your skillset; be very nice to

people but don't over-please people. Set
your standards.

- Stay fit and healthy because people are
more attracted to those who take good
care of themselves.
- To meet the right people, joining groups is
a good idea. Always find the right group
for the kinds of friends you want to make.
- To strengthen bonds, value the
connections you have made and spend
time with the friends you already have.

AFTERWORD

I am glad we made it to the end of the book. I hope by now you will be brimming with new confidence in your new skillset. I want to assure you that the techniques in this book are all techniques that I have counseled and taught many people for many years of practice.

I want to say a big thank you for coming with me this far on this journey! It's been an exciting and interesting experience for me, and I believe you also had a fun time learning all that was shared in this book.

When I was writing this book, I had you as a reader in mind and made the book as easy as possible so that both beginners and experts can benefit equally.

However, just reading the book won't be enough. You have to be practical to connect with other people. And like every other skillset, the more you practice, the more you will succeed. Therefore, I urge you to be open and willing to connect—then watch how your likability points change for the better.

The techniques are all proven to work, and there are many academic studies to back them; however, I have carefully selected the easiest methods that I have applied over the years.

I have taken the time to explain tested and proven tips that have worked for me and my friends. You have to understand the power of the first impression and make it work for you. People have less than a minute to decide if they like you or not. You also have to know how to employ simple nonverbal communication. It is a powerful tool in enhancing your relationships when meeting people.

People are naturally drawn towards similar persons; hence, this book has explained how to use this technique to make great friends. We have also discussed the importance of powerful small talk. You have to make the other party feel important by making the conversation about them. We have also discussed how to employ humor in lightening the mood when talking to people.

There is a section dedicated to being a friend yourself. This is the first and most important step in getting people to like you. You have to make efforts to work on yourself through personal hygiene and healthy lifestyle choices. When you are presentable and good-looking, people will be drawn to you. We have also dedicated a chapter to developing charisma. Developing charisma is more than being charming. It involves showing regard for people and being present during a conversation.

Remember not to tune out during a conversation, even if what the other person is saying is really boring and you desperately want to be elsewhere. Look at it this way: by giving this person your time you are showing, to others and yourself, that you can find the positives in anyone. That in itself is an attractive quality. So many people are quick to judge each other and focus on the negatives that it is refreshing when people come across a person who is genuinely positive and interested in everyone they meet. Persevere with that boring individual and you might find that they open up and reveal something deeper and a lot more interesting.

We have also examined the importance of self-confidence. This is reflected in many ways like the clothes we wear and our sense of purpose. In other words, you should have a goal and personal core values; this can be your driving force and personal principle that guides you every day. Developing your communication skills is also important. This involves guiding the conversation in the right direction and making others at ease with you.

Remember that making people like you is not fictional, magical, or an inborn gift. There are practical methods for you to become likeable after acquiring the skills necessary to engage people.

I believe that you have the potential to learn and master everything that is discussed in this book. Believe in yourself, commit to your daily practice, and you will attract many incredible friends who will stay with your for life.

Printed in Poland
by Amazon Fulfillment
Poland Sp. z o.o., Wrocław